YOU'RE INVITED...

THE EVOLUTION REVOLUTION: 2021

ARE YOU READY?

Self-Mastery for the Masses

Essays & Practices to Provoke,
Uplift, Inspire, Enlighten & Transform

S A H A R A

A SERVICE OF SIRIUS GALORE

First Edition: February 2021

ISBN: 978-1-7364652-0-2

Library of Congress Control Number: 2021900472

Cover art: Courtesy of NASA/Fermi Spirograph
Cover design: Sahara Devi

The Uplift & Inspire Collection © Sahara Devi
Available on etsy: https://www.etsy.com/shop/SiriusGalore

Printed in the United States of America

A Service of Sirius Galore
Bozeman. Montana

This book is dedicated to you—
the one in whose hands it is now.

I'm inviting you to take a journey with me,
a journey of awakening & discovery.
I've been preparing to be your guide on this journey
for more than half a century.

If you choose to avail yourself
of the Gifts being offered along the way,
you will find yourself emerging
like a butterfly from a cocoon,
and your life will be ever transformed.

So please read all the content in this book
from cover to cover,
because each step has been
carefully calibrated to bring you home
to your own Heart.

With Great Love,
Sahara

CHANGE YOURSELF & CHANGE THE WORLD:
IT'S AS SIMPLE AS THAT

I know you don't want to hear this:

The change you want to see can only come from the inside-out.

If you refuse to change yourself— you cannot change the world.

SAHARA
A SERVICE OF SIRIUS GALDAE

ARE YOU READY?

What if I told you that racial equality depends on you loving yourself unconditionally?

Or that the end of war depends on discovering your True Identity?

What if I told you that an unpolluted ocean requires you to let go of an old grudge?

Or that the end of homelessness depends on you taking out your earbuds, disconnecting from your device, and smiling at everyone you pass on the street?

What if, by recognizing that we are One—*and understanding that we are collectively responsible for all the good and all the ills we see in the world*—we each began to take personal responsibility for how that is?

And what if we understood that it all begins and ends with Love?

Everything you want to see:

Social Justice
Gender Equality
Sustainable Energy
People Over Profit
Clean Water, Air, Earth
Health & Well-being
Conscious Education
Peace & Harmony Among Peoples & Nations
Stewardship of Resources
Respect for All Life

Will only appear when enough of us choose to
invite
acknowledge
accept
embrace
focus on
cultivate
and express
our own
Higher Consciousness

COVID 2020: A CALL TO ARMS

With the elimination of so many distractions, have you now come face-to-face with yourself? Have you begun to question everything? Have you discovered what is really important?

A simple virus stopped us in our tracks and is wreaking havoc around the world—not because of some insidious global conspiracy, but because as a species we've been on a runaway train, speeding out of control in the wrong direction, and *something* had to happen to get our attention.

For not only have we been wantonly eviscerating the environment upon which we depend for our very existence, but we are mired in an appalling state of socioeconomic inequity, inequality, and injustice.

The thing is, it won't matter who we elect this year if enough of us don't change the quality of energy and consciousness we embody, and again scramble to restore the *status quo*. Something even more dramatic will have to show up to shock us into awakening and precipitate the necessary transformation of human civilization on planet Earth.

Because no amount of protest can accomplish what a simple shift in frequency and consciousness can, as protest by its very nature is anti-, and anti- simply embroils us in the static of the issue we are protesting.

And politics—which does a very good job of keeping us distracted and very well divided—is never the answer: righteousness cannot be legislated, goodness cannot be enacted into law, and greed cannot be criminalized.

In fact, the only true and lasting remedy against the forces of destruction running rampant, is a critical mass of enlightened consciousness permeating our Quantum Reality.

And that depends on you.

August 2020

AUTHOR'S NOTE

More than a decade has passed since the original *Evolution Revolution* (*The First Peaceful Revolution In The World — A Handbook for Personal & Global Transformation*) was published, and during the intervening period I have lived dozens of lifetimes—evolving apace.

So I have great hopes that the general population and potential readership has been experiencing their own evolutionary process and are ripe for the information asking to be shared in this new compilation.

For while I have noticed some interestingly enlightened shifts in the global village, the insanity of the Old Paradigm has intensified dramatically and is wreaking havoc with great vigor. The situation is both critical and dire.

To counter this alarming state of affairs, those of open heart and benevolent intention must seriously ramp up the quality of their game: for to be focused on the personal in the current circumstances is both irresponsible and extremely short-sighted at best. We cannot afford to be blasé about the planet and its inhabitants being devastated and demolished as we watch—and activism alone will not cut it.

Why?

Because we live in a Quantum Field—what we perceive as external reality is a direct reflection of our personal and collective consciousness—and in order to have sufficient juju to precipitate the transformation we desire to see in the world, we must each cultivate and firmly establish a more highly evolved Consciousness within.

This profound inner change can only be accomplished by equally profound desire, commitment, and devotion—and the dedication of our lives to the 'well-being of all.'

For those who may be reluctant to give unconditionally, fearing personal lack, know this: because we are inherently One, by serving the whole we are simultaneously serving our selves.

Please understand: the only true and lasting remedy against the forces of destruction running rampant is a critical mass of enlightened Consciousness permeating our Quantum Reality.

And that depends on you.

Bozeman, Montana
February 2020

FOREWORD

It may not be easy, but it's quite simple: If we want to change the world we have to change ourselves.

Each one of us.

In fact, it cannot happen in any other way.

The analogy I always use is the image of humanity as a single huge body, with each of us individual cells in that body. If our desire is to light up the body of humanity, we each of us have to light up our own cell.

We are One. Anything and everything we do as individuals is projected into the Quantum Field and instantly influences the fabric of reality. "If a butterfly flaps its wings in China, the effect is felt around the world."

So just imagine the collective emotional maelstrom—anger, fear, grief, envy, greed and malice—propelled into the energetic atmosphere in which we dwell. You can picture it as the proverbial, albeit energetic, shit-storm, raining down on the population every day, while people walk around wondering why they feel depressed, overwhelmed, frustrated, or enraged.

On top of that we have the programming of the media, sending waves of the same roiling emotional static into our personal energy fields through our radios, televisions, computers and cell phones—many even receiving this more directly into their brains through their earbuds.

What's a human to do?

It's really very simple: Since everything is energy—and energy vibrates at different frequencies—we begin by **choosing** the frequency we imagine we'd like to experience, and then doing whatever it takes to establish ourselves within that bandwidth.

And in the same way darkness cannot obliterate the Sun—it's always shining, behind every cloud or eclipse—a lower frequency cannot seriously affect an individual established in a higher vibration. For while it may be experienced like a shock wave (an attack of anxiety, grief, rage, or sudden depression) passing through the body in the same way an earthquake tremor is felt rolling through the ground, when we know ourselves as the Light we are, we acknowledge the energy for what it is, let it move on, and return to our default position: Awareness itself.

So here you go—a guide to Consciousness and Self-mastery—a primer for beginners, the curious, or those who consider themselves spiritual, but are still in judgment of the world around them.

INTRODUCTION

Albert Einstein is reputed to have said: "No problem can be solved from the same level of Consciousness that created it."

I say it this way: We cannot go beyond the mind with the mind.

This is the basis of our current challenge: we cannot think our way to the next level of being. The intellectual process is the antithesis of what is necessary here.

So what *is* necessary? First, to accept that there is something beyond what we have experienced and what we think—or in some cases believe—and to recognize that we are nowhere near the pinnacle of our development as human beings.

And then to understand that in the evolutionary process we are never completely in control; that the best we can do is position ourselves so that Consciousness has room to expand within us.

How does this happen? By beginning to shift our perspective from what we think, and think we know, to what can be perceived without the filter of the mind.

Right now, millions of people are awakening to the understanding that they are not who they believed themselves to be.

Unfortunately, sometimes it requires being beaten to a pulp before one is able to let go of that false identification. Equally unfortunate, worldly success sometimes interferes with this process, as ego-identification is often strengthened by that same success.

One may spend a lifetime meditating in a cave (actually or metaphorically) and still be unenlightened in one's daily life. This is because, although one has been given a glimpse of the Infinite, and has an intellectual understanding of That, one is still identified with the personality and thereby subject to human suffering. In other words, one can be intellectually aware of the Truth and still behave like a jerk.

A very simple exercise in self-awareness begins to take us beyond the identification with the persona that keeps us stuck in the illusion, and allows an opening for the Self to appear.

Welcome to the New Paradigm.

THE REVOLUTION & HUMAN ENLIGHTENMENT

When we speak of enlightenment, there is the capital E Enlightenment of a Ramana Maharshi—a happening, not something over which one has any control; a human flipped into a transcendent state by an inexplicable force—and then there is the enlightenment I am inviting you to embrace here: a state of Awareness humans are evolving into and able to achieve with intention.

This enlightenment has nothing to do with intellectual concepts—it is an experiential state that blooms as the result of desire and focus. It's not complicated, or even mystical—it's simply choosing to shift one's attention (and change one's behavior) in a way that enables one's own Higher Self to be more present in the body, and an awakened state of Consciousness to arise.

This doesn't require belief, just acceptance—but of course, one cannot accept without belief unless one experiences, and one cannot experience unless one chooses, and acts. It happens one step at a time: yearning, choosing, doing.

There are three components in the process:

Identity—Who do you think you are?
Frequency—Vibrating above the 3D turmoil
Self-mastery—Primarily, regarding thought (all else will follow)

Everything you need to proceed you are holding in your hands.

THE GREAT TRANSFORMATION: A WORLD AWAKENING (2017)

We are currently living in the most profoundly transformative time in the history of the Planet. Never mind the Industrial Revolution or even the advent of our current techno wonder-world: this is a time of Awakening Consciousness on a planetary level, and not one single being or location on Earth will remain untouched.

Of course, you may not be remotely aware of this, as we each experience life depending upon where we put our attention—and right now there is a reality show of international proportions grabbing the spotlight from nightly news to social media. However, those of us looking in another direction are perceiving an expansion in Consciousness of a Cosmic magnitude.

In 2008, after an unexpected 13-year sojourn 'living on the street' and being carried around the world with no-visible-means-of-support, I returned to Bozeman and wrote a little book called *The Evolution Revolution/The First Peaceful Revolution In The World, A Handbook for Personal & Global Transformation*. It was a work based on my own Awakening and recognition that "whatsoever we do to or for another, we are doing to or for our own selves—for good or ill." It spoke of a way of cultivating Self-Awareness and expanding Consciousness, and was published in the midst of the Great Recession—a crisis that demanded a rethinking of priorities and a recreating of systems. Unfortunately, rather than accept that uncomfortable truth and the accompanying challenge, the powers-that-be scrambled to recreate the *status quo* with all haste.*

In 2016 we experienced the consequences of those decisions with a vengeance—a nationwide dissatisfaction of such profound depth it led to an unprecedented rejection of establishment thinking and the elevation of an antihero into a position of power.

Meanwhile, the energetics of Transformation—not to be trifled with by out-of-control egos of any stature—are barreling on and showing up globally: from the astonishing upstart in the Vatican speaking a Christ-like rhetoric of caring for the poor, to alternative energy becoming a new norm, and governments around the world granting rights to animals, water and the Earth herself.

In all this we are witnessing what I call the Great Transformation: a period of societal upheaval and political antics indicating the death throes and approaching dissolution of the Old Paradigm on the one hand, and a greater acceptance of our interdependence arising in the multitudes, leading us toward a new way of being in Harmony with all life, on the other.

So where does that leave us as individuals, the 'little people,' who may feel powerless to have an impact in the face of such great turbulence? Where does the average Joe, a decent, hardworking, live-and-let-live kind of guy, who abhors how things are but doesn't have a clue what to do about it, find the power to make a difference if he is not a protester, activist, billionaire, celebrity or CEO?

If we are not simply reactive organisms, responding to stimuli like Pavlov's dogs, we have the profoundly influential power—and empowerment—of intentional, conscious choice. We can *choose* where to put our attention, we can *choose* what to feed with our energy, we can *choose* what to support with our money, we can *choose* how to respond to what we perceive, and we can *choose* the words and tone of voice in our speaking. We can *choose* the attitude and intention we bring into our world, and more specifically, our community.

It's actually quite simple: the key to the power of the individual, those who *en masse* make up the whole, is in relationship— because the basis of a harmonious life in any society depends upon our inter-relatedness and how we choose to treat those around us on a daily basis.

We needn't wait for a natural disaster to evoke a sense of 'all in this together' because we really *are* all in this—Life—together. We needn't wait for a catastrophe to inspire kindness, cooperation, consideration, generosity or compassion—*we can choose to embody those qualities and express them in every encounter*, every day—and race, religion, nationality, gender or even political affiliation need never come into play.

Start where you are. The simplest way to say it is: be friendly. And be kind. Such a simple thing.

We can choose to be friendly and pleasant when engaged in transactions with the cashier or waitress who serves us; we can choose to be considerate of others when we're driving down the street; we can choose to be kind, supportive or complimentary in every human transaction; and we can choose to smile at others for no reason at all—simply because they show up in front of us. In a world that has speeded up exponentially, just being willing to spend the moment it takes to be still and listen to what another wants to express is a kindness. **

All around us are folks working at jobs we've done, or jobs we would never want to do. These people are not nameless ciphers, they are our neighbors—someone's mother, father, sister, child or loved one—and they are *serving us* in the positions they occupy. What if we expressed appreciation for their service and made their encounter with us a moment of warmth and connection? *What if our default intention as we go about our daily life was making people feel good about themselves?* What if our speaking elicited the response: "You made my day." (My favorite phrase)

The change we want to see in our world is not something that can be legislated or imposed from without; it is not something we can achieve through protest. *It is something that can only come from within: each one of us choosing to bring a little more kindness into our way of being as we go about the business of living our lives.* Quantum physics tells us how the observer affects that which it observes— this is the way as individuals we affect our collective reality. What if we started to observe through the eyes of Love? In the same way that the reward of patience is patience, the reward of kindness is finding oneself living in a kind world. Verily: whatsoever we embody and express creates the world in which we live.

It's a question of critical mass. Small numbers have the power to affect collective consciousness and do, as when groups of TM meditators demonstrably reduced crime in cities by their focused practice. When we recognize we are part of a singular energetic field, and continuously contributing the quality of our energy to that unified field, we can begin to choose to embody and express more kindness—raising the vibratory rate of the collective and contributing to a transformed society.

Change yourself and change the world.

*The same thing is happening now (2021) in response to COVID. If we still don't get the message, I shudder to think what will show up next.

**Did you know that smiling releases serotonin? And that serotonin makes you feel good?

WHO DO YOU THINK YOU ARE?

How do you identify yourself?

By Race? Nationality? Gender? Education? Profession?

By what you have—or what you don't have?

Are you a victim of circumstance?

Scarred or maimed physically, psychologically, emotionally?

Imagine Life on Earth to be a board game:

We have a piece (body) to represent who we are. That piece then assumes a role.

We then proceed to move the piece around the board—according to a roll of the dice.

Some of the squares we land on have advantageous or beneficial outcomes; some are challenging or punitive. Some may be traumatic. We accumulate or lose possessions, have various adventures, and then the game is over.

Who is the one playing the game??

What would happen if an actor got so wrapped up in his role that he forgot his real identity?

If you're suffering, this is what happened to you. The character called _____ is just the role you're playing.

If you cease to identify with the role, the suffering will simply dissolve.

SAHARA
A SERVICE OF SIRIUS GALORE

THE TRAP OF 'SPIRITUALITY'

There are those that believe traditional religions confining, and that they have reached a higher level of existence by claiming to be spiritual rather than religious.

Unfortunately, many of these have only substituted one false identity for another more insidious one—convinced that to be spiritual is to be more advanced and somehow greater than the merely religious, and creating a false and detrimental sense of separation between themselves and others.

In fact, the popular concept of what it means to be spiritual can be both ignorant and arrogant—a trap set by the egoic mind instilling a subtle sense of smug satisfaction and superiority while simply creating a new, misleading, sense of self.

Don't be fooled by the cult of what is called spirituality. It's not by *adding* labels, techniques, practices, accomplishments or certifications—but by *eliminating everything that has been added*—until the original, indescribable Nature is revealed.

You *Are* That.

Know thy Self.

FYI

IN CASE YOU DIDN'T GET THE MEMO:

IT'S TIME TO INTEGRATE THE

HIGHER SELF

IT'S TIME—GET ON BOARD

What if our planet was at risk from a hostile force of space invaders (impervious to our weaponry) who intend to take over the world and turn us into slave-bots?

If there was a way to prevent this from happening, would you do whatever it takes?

Well, we are not being threatened by extra-terrestrial invaders, but by a cancerous force attacking the body of humanity from within.

Will you do what it takes to heal this dis-ease? Or have you not yet been personally affected enough to feel uncomfortable?

Because this is the situation: if you are feeling comfortable in your own personal life *and you're content to continue living in a self-centered way,* you are part of the problem—the problem that exists because not enough of us understand that we live in a Quantum Energy Field and every one of the almost 8 billion humans on the planet contribute their harmony or static to our quantum existence.

We are all at-effect-of everything that is happening everywhere. And—we are all *responsible for* everything that is happening to the whole.

So we cannot ignore the fact that there is sex-trafficking or female genital mutilation; or children separated from their mothers at our border; or torture and starvation; or the reprise of fascism, racism, and anti-semitism; or destruction of our environment, or pollution of our waters, or the extinction of species...

We cannot ignore the negative force that is attacking the body of humanity from within, simply because we are comfortable enough in our own privileged existence—for now.

But Old Paradigm solutions—that addressed the ills of the world from a strictly external perspective—are not what are going to work in this New Paradigm era.

The New Paradigm—operating from the availability of heightened frequencies of energy and expanded Consciousness—requires a collective refinement and attunement of our personal energy fields sufficient to uplift the whole of our Quantum existence.

And this means you.

If you are ready to do whatever it takes to heal the disease that is destroying the body of humanity, then:

YOU have to take responsibility for your contribution to the energetic soup we live in.

YOU have to step up your game, refine and upgrade your frequency, and align with your own Higher Self.

YOU have to stop thinking personally, and begin to think as a single cell in the body of humanity—understanding that the greater the Consciousness embodied by you, the greater the Consciousness contributed to the whole.

YOU have to understand that we are all in this together—and that if YOU don't begin living for the well-being of all, WE are all going down the tubes together.

If you are ready to do whatever it takes to heal the disease that is destroying the body of humanity, then please begin right now.

Discard all the programming
Remove all the apps

Push the reset button
Return to default
Restore original blueprint

Discover who you are

PLEASE—WAKE THE F$%K UP

'Wakethefuckup' is the name of a FB page I stumbled upon, and while I may not agree with all its posts, I wholeheartedly appreciate the sentiment: *Wake the f&%k up.*

If you haven't realized what's actually going on, we're in a societal healing crisis and we're witnessing what I call the 'death throes of the old paradigm.' *We are experiencing the most profoundly transformative chapter in human history, and the most dramatic up-shift in Consciousness that has ever occurred on the Planet.*

Life can no longer be lived from a personal point of view—we are One, and needs must **consider ourselves and function as part of the whole.**

We are being nudged, gently and/or violently (depending on the status of personal Consciousness and location on the planet) out of complacency, and if we have any kind of clue we'll respond. But how?

If you're action-oriented, you're certainly welcome to march, protest, or 'resist' in any way you see fit—but the heart and foundation of the issue is the need to make a conscious, deliberate shift in Consciousness—and it's a continuing process.

If you think you're already on the spiritual path and that makes you okay, you may simply be dreaming you're awake. Yes, you may be 'enlightened' to a modest degree, but you may also only be operating from a new, improved, spiritual ego: WTFU

If you're gadding about, nicely fixed, content with your lot, not personally affected by the insanity rampaging like a wild-fire through our society; if you think you've nothing left to learn, your life is not wanting, your needs are met, you don't have to struggle—your arrogance may come back to bite you in the ass and your smugness will certainly be humbled in one way or another. WTFU

What to do? Ask. Out loud, (HELP!!!) or silently within. Ask the Universe, (or whatever/whomever you relate to—your own Higher Self, your 'Guardian Angel,' or any enlightened Being or Deity) to reveal what *you* need to know to move onto the next step of your personal evolutionary process. It won't matter to whom you address yourself—you *will* get a response if you're sincere in your request. WTFU

If you think this is all hocus-pocus, take it as a challenge: Ask your own subconscious to open your eyes and ears so you are able to see and hear what has yet been unseen or unheard—and while you're at it, ask for your inner senses to be awakened as well. WTFU

Then, of course, you have to be alert and aware of the subtle messages that come as a response. *And follow them.* Because what's the point of asking for direction and ignoring the answers if they don't conform to your desires?

It is certainly obvious that we cannot continue as we have been.

Please: Wake The F&%k Up.

ON 'MAKING YOUR DREAMS COME TRUE'

Many teachers of 'self-improvement' attract paying customers by advertising seminars that focus on *Making Your Dreams Come True*. These "award-winning authors and internationally acclaimed consultants and seminar leaders" say they will help you:

Take-home Tools for Personal Happiness
Go for (and Get) What You Want
Effortlessly Achieve Focus, Happiness and Success
Be a Psychic in a Day
Set your mind to achieve the life you really, really want
And even: *Make money with self-improvement seminars!*

I'm here to share a different message:

We no longer have time for self-indulgence.

We cannot indulge in our personal desires while one out of every six of us lives in poverty and hunger. Rather than a personal dream or the American Dream, we need to focus on a *collective dream*: A dream of Transformation that we make a reality. The evolutionary transformation that will take us from the paradigm of power, manipulation and greed, to the understanding of our Oneness and the behaviors that result from being whole-heartedly invested in the well-being of all.

How is this possible? By transcending the limited, false concept of self based on identification with body/mind/personality, and moving into the expanded Awareness of one's True Nature.

We've been programmed to believe that satisfaction (and success) comes from the clothes we wear, the phone we use, the car we drive, where we dine, the power we wield, who we know, and especially: how much money we have in the bank.

I'm here to tell you otherwise: You are not your clothes, your phone, your connections, etc. You are not your job—it's just a role you play. You are not your mental capacity, however erudite or ignorant. You are not your personality, however dull or scintillating.

What are you? An expression of All-That-Is—an aspect of Source. A manifestation of Consciousness. A single cell in the body of Humanity. An Embodiment of Love.

Don't be afraid. You will not lose yourself. Pleasure does not cease. On the contrary, all the senses are heightened, all experience becomes more delightful, and one is filled from the inside out.

All that disappears is the suffering, and the sense of separation.

Are you ready for that? Good.

We don't have to do big things.
There are BILLIONS of us.
If we all did little things
every day
that would be a heckuva big thing.

THE GREAT TRANSFORMATION & YOU

If you are ready to move into the New Paradigm, if you choose to participate in the Great Transformation—moving out of concern for the personal self and joining forces with the Legions of Light currently engaged in elevating an entire Planet into a Higher Realm of being—your life will begin to change in ways both joyful and profound.

As you consciously work on elevating your own frequency—in the name of service, for the well-being of All—you first receive the benefits of the intention of your dedication. For the higher the frequency of your energy body, the greater the synchronicity in your field, and the more ease and grace in your life.

The more you choose to move beyond the personal into the Universal—the Oneness—the more aligned you become and the more de-Light-ful your experience.

The higher your frequency, the more Light you carry; the more Light you carry, the greater the effect you have on those around you—elevating the frequency of your environment, and the community in which you reside or the arenas in which you move. As everything gets better for everyone, it naturally gets better for you.

Realize you are not alone in this work—but part of a great wave of Consciousness that is focused on and influencing the Planet, elevating and transforming the very fabric of reality.

Be not distracted by the shenanigans of various actors in the play—each one has her part. Simply play your own role with dedicated focus, and watch the changes that arise before your eyes—they are happening, now, everywhere.

The appearances of Time & Space are mutable, not fixed. What you call 'miracles' are simply manifestations at a higher level of being, and child's play for Masters who can manipulate energy at will.

But this is a collective endeavor, and if you would **be part of it** you must **take part in it**—else the state of *our* union will remain chaotic and distressful.

Just choose. Step on board.

You will be supported in ways you cannot even imagine.

WHAT CAN ONE 'NOBODY' DO?
THE POWER OF ONE

*The Power of One is the fact that we are each **a vital cell** in the body of humanity, and as an individual, have the power—and responsibility—to be an important contribution to the Quantum Field in which we exist, thereby improving everything for everybody.*

The Power of One tells us that what we perceive as reality 'out there' is the direct result of what we as individuals project into the collective soup of our existence—and that the way to change what we don't like out there, is to change the quality of **our** contribution, period.

So what can one 'nobody' do? More than you can imagine…

In this currently schizophrenic society, where too often the answer to the question "What do you want to be when you grow up?" is "a celebrity," it's vital to understand the power of the well-intentioned individual.

The position we are in at this moment—on the brink of Planetary Awakening—*calls for all those open to the possibility of change to manifest their desire for that into the world.* We are each placed in the perfect position to play the role we were born to play—which has nothing to do with a 'job' or position, and everything to do with carrying Light and embodying Love.

You don't have to be a celebrity to have a significant impact on the world at large—*you simply have to start acting in an impactful manner*. While in the eyes of the world you may not be renowned, in the eyes of Source you are anything but an anonymous cipher—so don't act that way, and don't treat others as such. *Each one of us is an aspect of All-That-Is, playing our role in this Cosmic Play.*

Life, as energetic impulse, happens locally and spreads like ripples out into the greater reality. When you choose to be an intentional Bearer of Light and begin to shine your Light on those around you, they too Light up and the pay-it-forward effect is ignited. Once enough of these small sparks are burning, the effect can be as great as a raging wildfire. *Now is the time to contribute to the critical mass needed to tip the scales.*

The key is feeling: embodying the Love we are, *choosing* to feel good, and transmitting that good feeling to everyone we encounter. It also requires us to slow down—and not allow ourselves to be rushed by the 'hurry up' energy all around us.

This is how it works:

I shop at various stores around town and interact with cashiers, produce workers, managers. I go to the Library, the Post Office, the bakery, the local newspaper. I use a printing service, an auto shop; I may encounter a janitor, waitress, executive. I frequent a yarn store, an optician's, a card shop, a bank.

Some of the people who work in these places or positions are known to me, some are friends, some become friends through our interactions, some not. It doesn't matter how well I know them, or if I know them at all—some of my most delightful exchanges happen when I talk to a 'stranger' while waiting in line for a cashier.

In any instance, rather than an impersonal, detached or perfunctory attitude, I *choose* to be friendly for starters, and with every encounter up the ante: express appreciation; offer a compliment; make a *sincere* inquiry into well-being; initiate an exchange of meaningful conversation, encouragement, inspiration, support.

*I act like these people have value in my life **because they do***: they are the community of Love I am building around me day by day with every encounter.

And I am also willing to listen, receptively, when the other has something they want heard. In fact, sometimes the greatest gift we can give another being is to simply be willing to take the time to listen to what they want to express.

This attitude, and intention—of *choosing* to be a transmitter of the Love frequency—is how each of us can affect the community around us and have an impact on our world. ***The high-quality frequency of your energy alone is the greatest contribution you can make***.

So please stop thinking you're a 'nobody'—you are somebody who has a great deal to offer if you choose to play the role you're here to play: bringing the Love you are to every encounter.

And once you begin, you'll see how powerful an impact you can have by a very obvious sign: the people you've begun to share a little Love with, will smile when they see you coming.

How does it get any better than that!?!

CRITICAL MASS

Have you ever popped popcorn in a pot on a stove? It starts off slowly—one lonely kernel, a signal. Gradually more join in until it reaches the point where the kernels are popping almost all at once—rapid-fire.

We're in the early stages of that process in terms of the awakening of Consciousness on the Planet—those who are more interested in "transforming the fabric of reality for the well-being of all," than self-enrichment, self-aggrandizement or self-promotion—are awakening and recognizing two profound truths: *We are One & there's enough* and, *Our time has come.*

We are One and there's enough. There are enough resources and enough know-how to create a world that is pollution-free and providing abundantly for all its inhabitants. The sticking point is the desire for power, and greed. In order to change that the Hundredth Monkey* effect has to kick in. And that depends on you—your *active* participation.

The analogy used in the Foreward applies here: If we want the body of humanity to be enlightened, each of us needs to focus on enlightening our own cell. The more of us who light up our cells, the Lighter the body will be. That 'Light' is awakened Consciousness, and critical mass in terms of social engineering is a much smaller number than we imagine—according to Gregg Braden, somewhere between 10-17%.

Our time has come. We have reached the point where the process of awakening Consciousness is being supported on a mass scale—by Cosmic forces of Universal proportion—and whether you know it or not, if you're reading these words, you are meant to participate in this glorious transformation of a civilization and a planet.

You're not being asked to make any sacrifices, and you're not being asked to spend money you may not have. You're only being asked to step forward and proclaim: "I'm in. I'm willing to take the simple steps that will enable Consciousness to more fully awaken in me. I'm willing to cultivate Love in my own being and generate that Love into my community in order to uplift humanity and transform the fabric of reality for the well-being of all."

Get on board—it's the ride of a lifetime.

* An anecdotal example of Collective Consciousness or Universal Mind

HUMANITY'S CHALLENGE—2019*

"The body is everywhere assaulted by all of our new media, a state which has resulted in deep disorientation of intellect, and destabilization of culture throughout the world."

Eric McLuhan

Humans today have an extraordinary challenge—and it has nothing to do with climate change or anything else you may imagine to be of great import—because most of you do not perceive past the illusion that has been carefully woven about you by those who would retain the *status quo*.

This critical challenge is whether or not you will allow yourselves as a race to be co-opted by technology and the devices it uses to distract you from a Higher Reality, and proceed to live as extensions of, and tethered to, those devices—or,

If enough of you will awaken enough, and choose to align with your True Nature—making the choice to live in a balanced and harmonious way with each other, the animals, birds, sea creatures and Earth herself—supporting the well-being of all.

These two pathways lead to two very different outcomes, and the choice must be made now. Not to put too fine a point on it—you are way past the Eleventh Hour: evidence the travesty playing out on the world stage. And make no mistake, your politicians cannot save you—this is a boots-on-the-ground, all-in-it-together, critical-mass-required call-to-arms.

✧ ✧ ✧

The first pathway, currently most evident, derives from the use of technology and its attendant devices that attract you as toys attract children: they fascinate and distract, sucking you into a world where you are manipulated into believing there is value where there is nothing but smoke and mirrors.

And that is their function: to lure you into an illusory world—a world even termed *virtual reality*—where you can pretend you are something you are not and live life as if it were a game you can win by accumulating points, or likes.

This unconscious trance—that you have allowed yourselves to be programmed into by the marketing industry and your media—has you believing that you are limited, finite creatures, subject to what appears to be the trials and tribulations of life on Earth, and making you imagine that—whatever they are selling in the moment—will fulfill you.

While this trance allows you to believe that you are living in an advanced civilization, the state of humanity today is closely analogous to your 'cavemen' in terms of the only capacity that counts—Consciousness—simply transposed onto what you consider to be modern society.

What you do not recognize in your dream-state, is that a civilization steeped in competition, war, might-makes-right, deprivation and depravity, greed, and the destruction of other species and the environment, are all signs of a very primitive way of life indeed.

And unfortunately, even much of what passes for so-called spirituality in your society today is often another form of distraction, lulling many into believing they are on a higher path when they are simply engaged in another level of self-delusion.

This pathway will lead to a world where humans become more and more reactive and machine-like in their behavior and responses, almost merged with their devices, and literally programmed to function in service to society in an extreme version of the economic machine that exists today.

The second pathway is that of awakening out of this dream-state you've been conditioned into, recognizing the Oneness of Life, and proceeding to live in accordance with that understanding.

This means, that as an individual, you realize that the way you choose to live—your attitude, your intentions, and your every act—is either in alignment with the well-being of all and enhancing your collective reality, or simply self-serving.

Once you are willing to look at yourself objectively, and make the deliberate choice to live in alignment with your own True, Higher Nature, you begin to adjust yourself in attitude, intention and behavior so that you contribute all you are, all you have, and all you do, to and for that 'well-being of all.'

Then, when enough of you choose this way of being, aligning your energetic frequencies with that of an elevated Consciousness, everything you want to change in your world will happen with very little effort, as all of the knowledge to make those changes is either already available, or accessible through connection to Cosmic Mind—and with the elimination of self-serving can come about with ease.

The last hurdle that needs overcoming in taking this step is the fear that, by sharing all you have and are and do with others, you will somehow not have enough for yourself.

What you may not understand is that by choosing to be an open channel through which you are continuously contributing to the whole, you cannot possibly deprive yourself of anything, as, being an integral part of the whole, that open channel is receiving from every contribution being made, and beyond—it's an energetic flow.

So, if you have children or grandchildren or want them, (or are simply a good, decent human being), and you'd like the world to be a place where Nature and all life is respected and protected, and where nations live in Harmony and Peace, then this is the time to take a definitive step into the New Paradigm calling for your participation, and out of the old self-centered and self-serving concepts of the previous centuries.

The upshot being: you either recognize that the well-being of all is the highest path and align yourself in its service, or you continue to focus on your own small needs and desires, and fiddle away as the global Rome burns to the ground.

The entire Universe is available in your support, and awaiting your answer.

How will you respond?

*Note: While most of this writing comes through me as a flow rather than being a product of the intellect, this was a very clearly 'channeled' message.

21ST CENTURY ENLIGHTENMENT

The 21st Century enlightenment process is not at all the same as either the 20th Century version or that which came before.

The 21st Century has brought the planet a huge influx of high-frequency energy—which has been intensifying as the years progress; reached the knock-your-socks-off stage to empaths at the onset of 2019; and will soon be jacked up to the cannot-be-avoided level—obvious to all.

If you're feeling out-of-sorts, experiencing frustration, or uncomfortable in any way, this is why: it's like going from sea-level to the Himalayas—the oxygen is thinner, and you have to acclimate yourself to the new conditions.

(Of course, your experience of this will depend upon your sensitivity and the level of Consciousness at which you are currently functioning, and you may not realize that some subtle sense of discomfort is actually due to this factor and not about you personally.)

While previously one sat, with the desire and intention of stilling the body and quieting the mind—so that Awareness might arise and Consciousness be experientially present—the conditions have now been established that invite us to exist in full, eyes-open, boots-on-the-ground Consciousness, bringing that Awareness into all our relationships and activities.*

We don't need special rooms to provide a setting, or any particular paraphernalia to facilitate a practice—we embody everything needed and carry that conscious-frequency into the world around us, being the energetic agents of change we came here to be.

The foundation for such an Awareness is the self-mastery required to reach the point of no longer being at-effect-of one's thoughts. Without that mastery, one is simply spinning one's wheels, stuck in a false identity, be it so-called spiritual or otherwise.

Because as long as we identify as a particular human something, anything, we are still choosing the limitation of whatever that is and not the unlimited state of Consciousness itself in a body, which requires no definition and has no limitation.

So if you would consciously avail yourself of the extraordinary opportunity existing on the planet at this time for your benefit (those frequencies which are upgrading everything in the biosphere and ushering in the New Paradigm on offer to humanity) I invite and encourage you to step into the self-mastery you are meant to embody.

*You understand, of course, that what is called meditation is not *something one does*, but a state that arises when one provides the appropriate environment within for it to happen, yes?

POINT OF INFORMATION—RE: EGO

Ego is simply a case of mistaken identity.

What is called ego is a symptom—indicating there is identification with the organism/attributes rather than the True Nature, resulting in an aberration of thought processes and behavior, with emotional and psychological reactions to what-is.

Once the frequency of the personal energy field is raised sufficiently, and enough pure Consciousness permeates the organism, the attachment to and identification with the body/personality subsides, and the identification rightfully reverts to, and abides in, Consciousness Itself.

At that time, as the mistaken identification recedes, emotional/psychological reactions diminish or dissolve, depending on the degree of Consciousness embodied. This eliminates the distorted thinking and behavior—and the suffering—that has resulted from the previous *mésalliance*, and enables the being to experience and express as the Consciousness it is.

The symptom no longer presents.

The True Nature reigns.

The sooner the more of us
stop identifying
with the attributes
of the organism,

the sooner
that which divides us
will disappear

ON THE 'MIND'

What we call 'mind' has no real existence. We have thoughts (that arise), and we have thinking—practical and intentional (a function of the brain), and we have Consciousness (the field of Higher Self). What we call mind is connected to the false sense of self (persona/ego), because when we are aligned with Consciousness, mind is not present—only Awareness exists.

When we are identified with the false sense of self—the small, limited persona—we are tossed about by the thoughts that arise and trapped in a perpetual (e)motion machine with no resolution. Hence psychotherapy—an endless dwelling on/analysis of thoughts that arise, and emotions provoked by same.

I remember Werner Erhard (1975) saying: the function of mind is to perpetuate its own existence. And I would say: what we call mind is simply the result of being lost in, and at-effect-of, the thoughts that arise.

Perhaps it's time to put an end to the idea of 'mind' and simply choose to experience ourselves as Awareness: pure perception both through, and beyond, the senses. In this way we free ourselves to experience the vastness of our Being, and lose/loosen the shackles of confinement to a mind that does not actually exist.

You cannot call yourself 'spiritual'
if you
complain, criticize or pass judgment.

You are only rooted
in your Spiritual beingness
if you allow Heart-centered consciousness
to inform
your speaking & behavior

ON SPIRITUALITY (GET OVER YOURSELF)

If you think that spirituality is a matter of sitting in meditation for x amount of time per day; if you think that by using a *mala* and repeating a *mantra*—or any other practice you may have—is what makes a being spiritual or defines spirituality, you are sadly mistaken. These practices may make you an *aspirant*, but in and of themselves, they do not make you spiritual.

(Naturally, I am not speaking of those monks whose entire lives are dedicated to cultivating and embodying high frequency energy for the benefit of humanity.)

Those practices, while considered by egos to be superior to the practices of those who engage in religion, are actually of the same ilk—although they may or may not include the adoration of a particular deity or representation of same. In fact, very often, what has occurred is simply the shifting from worldly ego to spiritual ego, a sorry condition merely amplifying one's delusion and not at all conducive to actually embodying the attributes of Spirit.

True spirituality is not a practice but a state of being in tune with the Truth of existence. To be spiritual is to be connected to Life through the Heart, to know—not intellectually, but existentially—one's connectedness to All-That-Is, *and to embody and express that in your daily life.*

It occurs with an increase in the frequency of one's energy field, and results in *incorporating the attributes* of Spirit, or Higher Consciousness, into the human expression.

Spirituality, or what may more accurately be termed: the integration of Higher Consciousness, or one's Higher Self, is in fact an extremely practical boots-on-the-ground application.

Yes—there's an app for that. But it's not found in any App Store and unfortunately, there is no online game that you can play and practice your skills. Those skills must be honed and then exercised from moment to moment in day-to-day life: observing every thought one thinks and all the self-talk in which one engages; capital A Awareness in every encounter and conversation; monitoring one's basic attitude about living, and one's behavior in relating to the world-at-large. The integration of Higher Consciousness is a very big endeavor—and the reason we're here: to embody that individually and be a part of a collective contribution to the transformation of the world.

The embodying of one's True Self, or integrating Higher Consciousness, can begin with an epiphany: the recognition that there is something more than the 3D experience to which we're accustomed—or an aspiration: the longing for something greater, or higher, that one eventually understands is actually another aspect of oneself. This longing then becomes an intention, and as one evolves, consciously choosing how one wishes to be, subsequently begins to be expressed in application—raising one's frequency in the process and enabling more of that aspect to reside in the body as the ego-identity diminishes and dissolves.

But the process of embodiment requires constant practice, and is where boots-on-the-ground comes into play—because that practice is not done in isolation. While it's relatively easy to create inner peace sitting in a cave, or in a special room arranged to facilitate serenity and concentration, the real work is done in the world, on the street, every day—where life is actually lived.

In the same way that physical muscles are toned by physical exercise, the muscles of Consciousness are toned by cultivating Self-Awareness, (not to be confused with self-awareness, an attribute of *homo-sapiens*), which is a much more demanding process than one may imagine is implied by the term.

✧ ✧ ✧

Self-Awareness is *invited* by acute, persistent observation of one's thoughts, speaking and actions, and gradually evolves into a state of being: acting, speaking, thinking and observing simultaneously, while the identity rests in the Consciousness.

This is not something that happens overnight. The ability to refrain from engaging in the thoughts that arise is a PhD level achievement. Eventually however, one has integrated sufficient Awareness to refrain from engaging in or responding to those constantly arising thoughts while going about one's daily life, and functions in a Self-directed, rather than self-directed, manner.

And while we are told and may imagine that we have free will—until a certain level of Consciousness is embodied, and one has mastered the ability to spontaneously observe/monitor and *choose* both thought and speech, most of what is called free-will is simply a kind of Pavlovian reaction to what shows up in one's environment based on one's mental, psychological, and emotional conditioning.

Free-will can only be exercised when we are Aware and Self-Aware enough to be making true conscious choice in any given situation.

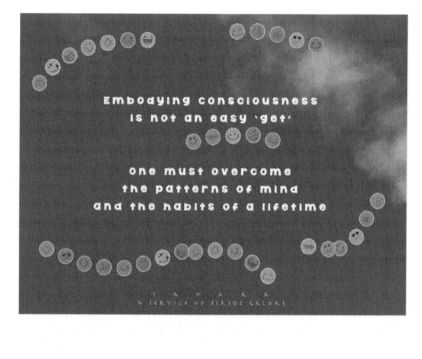

Embodying consciousness
is not an easy 'get'

one must overcome
the patterns of mind
and the habits of a lifetime

TAHARA
A SERVICE OF SIRIUS GALORE

FEAR V. LOVE

What drives you?

Are you centered in your Heart and willing to give without needing compensation?

Or are you afraid that if you give freely you will not have enough for yourself?

This fear—driven by lack of Trust, is what holds the world in thrall. It exists because much of humanity has been trained to believe in scarcity, when in fact there is Infinite Abundance.

Not just the abundance that exists on the planet—which is legion—but an abundance that transcends the material and can appear out of the ethers in the blink of an eye.

The one writing these words has had repeated demonstrations of physical money appearing for her in what would be called a miraculous way. By this, and other manifestations of fulfillment when there has been need, she has been trained in Trust, and trained to give freely without fear of lack.

This is what you are all now being called to do: Give freely.

✧ ✧ ✧

How many of you have stated, or agree with the statement, "Be the change?"

And how many of you have had the courage to fully walk that talk?

If you claim a desire to change the world, yet you are not prepared to change yourself in order to accomplish that, how do you imagine it will happen?

Contrary to the modern fascination with and celebration of a veritable pantheon of super-heroes, in reality they are not waiting in the wings or on call to save the day. And if you think your politicians have the ability to do so you are sadly mistaken—each one of you must contribute to the change you desire by your own metamorphosis: YOU are the superhero in this story.

The metamorphosis necessary will take you from the limited character you think you are, to the Infinite Being you are in Truth. And Infinite Beings have no fear of giving freely—they are connected to an Infinite Source.

So practice your infinitude by giving freely.

Because you exist in a Quantum Reality—where an energetic unified field connects all of humanity—and humanity's collective consciousness is what drives the *appearance* of your 3D world, *the only way the change you desire will occur is when enough of you begin to embody the qualities you claim to admire.*

Give freely.

When you do, you inspire others to do the same. It's that pay-it-forward/ripple effect—that has the potential to spread unceasingly.

It may be compared to a siphon: once the flow begins it continues as long as there is substance to draw from. And since this is an Infinite Universe with an inexhaustible source of energy, there is no end to the available substance.

Give freely.

And understand that the Truth expressed by the terms Quantum Reality and Unified Field is a collective Oneness. You are part of a whole, and by benefitting any part of that whole you are benefitting yourself, and hastening the transformation you long for.

Give freely.

You will never lack for anything essential if you do—and your life will become quite Divine.

On Giving

The only things we actually 'have' are those we are willing to give — having without giving is like inhaling without exhaling: only half the story.

Giving is always a one-way flow — the concept of 'energy exchange' being created by those unable to give freely. Always give with no thought of return. We are not cups that can be emptied — we are rivers that flow one-way into the ocean of Life. A river flows without thinking — it is connected to an infinite Source.

Puttaparthi/September 1999

IGNORE EVERYTHING

If you were a vegan at a buffet, would you fill your plate with ribs, sausages & organ meats? Wouldn't that be ridiculous?

Now let's imagine that we desire not only to transform the world into a place of abundance for all, peaceful co-existence and respect for all forms of life, but we wish ourselves to be expressions of our highest Divine potential, living in Harmony with ourselves and others.

If this were true, why would we spend our time and energy involved in and provoked by all we consider to be undesirable?

Isn't it absurd to think about, talk about, dwell on and obsess about—all that we don't desire?

Yes. It is. Absurd and counter-productive.

This includes the news—online, print, radio and TV, which all do a superlative job of keeping us distracted from what we would like to see manifest. No—you don't need to be 'informed.' Not if you wish to be part of the enlightened host of Beings who are willing to do what it takes to create the world we desire. Nonetheless, everything you actually need-to-know will be made known to you.

IGNORE EVERYTHING except what you desire in your reality.

Focus on that.

✧ ✧ ✧

We don't create change by concentrating on the undesirable, and *fighting* for change. We create change by *choosing to be, express, model and demonstrate exactly what we do desire.*

You want more Love in the world? Be more Loving.

You want more compassion in the world? Be more compassionate.

You want more generosity in the world? Be more generous.

You want to be an agent of change?

IGNORE EVERYTHING—*except what you desire in your reality.*

Focus on, and be a model of, that.

Ch♥♥sing t♥ engage

in the current imbr♥gli♥

Is like ch♥♥sing t♥ sit in a sewer

and bathe in the stink

Why w♥uld y♥u want t♥ d♥ that?

THE GLORIFICATION OF BUSY

"Are you keeping busy?" I'm asked.
"No," I answer, "I'm not interested in being busy."

When did busy become so desirable?

Busy is a distraction—a concept fostered by a capitalist culture, that would have you so engaged in chasing the illusive satisfaction always dangling just out of reach, that you have no time to look around and realize you're a rat on a treadmill—moving quickly, going nowhere.

Busy leaves no time for being, for contemplation, for asking the important questions and getting the answers that move one into a realm where satisfaction reigns and busy is no longer attractive or desirable.

The state of busy keeps us from being still, and actually experiencing what we are: Consciousness in a body. And people fear stillness because they have not achieved mastery over their thoughts or thinking—and are mostly not aware of the possibility of doing so.

Stillness is a threat to the part that doesn't know who or what it is.

The art of stillness, once achieved, is not simply that of the body, it also includes a quiescent mind: the ability to ignore arising thoughts that distract and create an agitation that leads the persona to busy-ness.

The mastery over thought enables an inner stillness even in the midst of activity—so one can be anywhere, doing anything, and rest in one's serene Awareness regardless of what is occurring in one's environment.

I love the stillness. Out of stillness comes inspiration, and creativity. In stillness is contentment, peace, and Love.

Be still, and know—I Am That.

The whole world is urging you:
"hurry up, hurry up"

Your own breath entreats you:
"slow down, slow down"

S A H A R A
A SERVICE OF SIRIUS GALORE

NO FEAR

A long, long time and umpteen lifetimes ago, I was involved with a particular teacher. One night I had one of those dreams that is not just a psychological construct:

I was standing on a fragment of a stone wall suspended in space. It was daytime—Sun, shining; sky, blue.

This teacher was suspended in space about thirty feet away from me, and he gestured for me to come to him.

I gestured back: "How am I supposed to get there?"

He just repeated the gesture to come.

Again I gestured: "There's nothing between us to support me."

Again he gestured: "Come." This time I decided to go for it.

(Remember the Indiana Jones movie where Indy has to leap across a chasm and a bridge appears as he does so?)

A similar thing happened to me: as I extended my foot to step off the wall, a stepping-stone appeared to support me.

Ever since then, I have never failed to step into the unknown fearlessly—knowing that whatever support I require will be there when I need it.

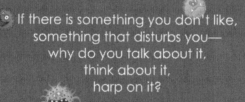

If there is something you don't like,
something that disturbs you—
why do you talk about it,
think about it,
harp on it?

It's like eating something that makes you sick.
If something makes you sick

STOP EATING IT

A SERVICE OF SIRIUS GALORE

COMPLAINT & CRITICISM:
YOU'RE MAKING YOURSELF SICK

Are you a constant critic? Find yourself complaining about the weather, the state of the world, the behavior of whomever?

You're making yourself sick.

Previously, I wrote about the fact that your complaints and criticism were affecting the whole: because we are One, connected in a Quantum Field, whatsoever you express into that field contributes to the quality of energy contained in it.

To that end, I suggested you beware your speaking— because by criticizing what you **don't** like 'out there' you are contributing the static of that criticism to that collective energy field, and are actually part of the problem you dislike.

*The most effective way to change what we don't like, is by creating more of the quality of energy **we do like**. This requires the discipline of focus on the desirable, while still being aware of, but essentially ignoring, the undesirable.*

(Naturally, this does not include the activists, who are playing the role of activism. And if there is an *action* you wish to take, by all means, do so.)

What I neglected to mention at that time was the effect that speaking would have on the individual personally.

In my previous handbook, *The Evolution Revolution/The First Peaceful Revolution in the World*, I provide three exercises in awareness: regarding thought, speaking and behavior. In describing the effect of speaking/behavior I explain that whatever you direct toward another, for good or ill, *first passes through you* before it reaches the other. And I suggest you are doing yourself harm with your anger, antagonism, etc. As so eloquently expressed by Proust: *Resentment is like drinking poison and expecting the other person to die.* *

An example I often use to clarify the quality of energy expressed by different frequencies, is the very obvious difference between a lullaby and heavy metal music. A lullaby may be equated to an expression of Loving, kindness or caring—while heavy metal may be likened to aggression, antagonism, or violence. So just imagine the effect of these disparate qualities on the energy field, not to mention the very cells, of your body. The one would be soothing, even healing, while the other would cause disturbance, distress, and perhaps even destruction. (See Emoto's Messages From Water)

Now complaint and criticism, while not obviously violent, are nevertheless destructive in the same way that water continually moving over stone is destructive: the constant pressure of the water wears away the stone. Complaint and criticism are low-grade frequencies, and their continual usage has a low-grade deleterious effect on the body itself and all aspects of the being.

 Do you have any strange symptoms of dis-ease in your body? Things that can't be explained medically? Or maybe you feel 'depressed'? Perhaps it would behoove you to be aware of your speaking, and the quality of the energy that is expressing through your mouth.

At this point, if you still need a good reason to refrain from the kind of speaking that contributes to the distressing *status quo* of society, reflect on this: the quality of energy you are expressing is affecting the very cells of your body—you could be making yourself sick with your own words.

—> or thoughts

*I'm hoping that you're already aware that the thoughts you think affect your body, and your experience, but I'm not addressing that here.

*Clearing waste out of your
mental and emotional bodies
is as important as
moving your bowels.*

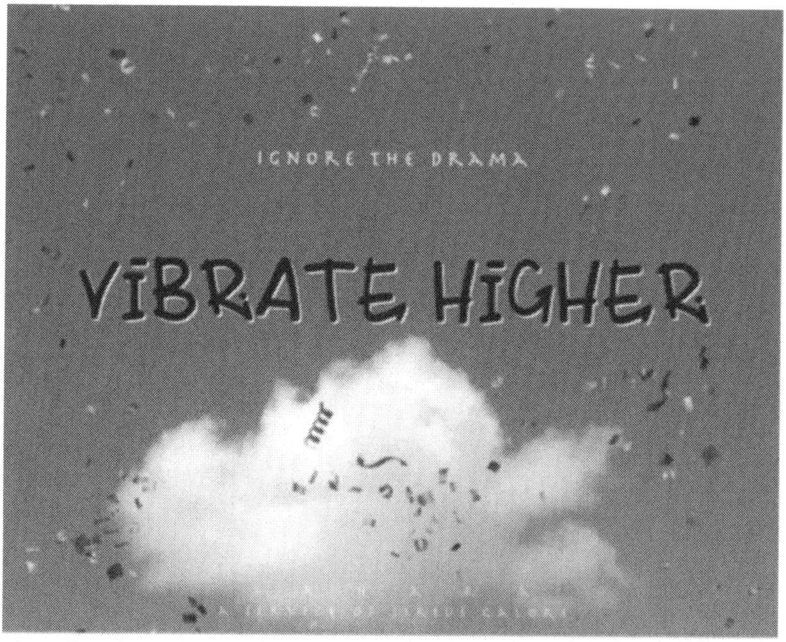
IGNORE THE DRAMA
VIBRATE HIGHER

EMOTIONAL DRAMA

It's like being a junkie.

Those who are consciously or unconsciously addicted to the drama, the intrigue, the excitement or disturbance of dramatic emotional energy, have firmly embroiled themselves in the insanity of the 3D reality playing out on the world stage. It feeds them like a drug, regardless of any judgment they may have in opposition to the storyline.

To rise above that maelstrom of energy and dwell in the realm of centered Consciousness, it requires a staunch Heart and dedicated focus, as the collective emotional environment is something like quicksand—always pulling at and sucking in those who are not mindful enough to remain quiescent.

If you've had enough of emotional turbulence, and you'd like to kick that addiction—which creates stress in your body, mind, and spirit—the way out is through your Heart.

The Heart is the center of connection and direction. Your Heart is the eye of the hurricane: a calm, still haven at the center of your being.

✧ ✧ ✧

When you feel yourself getting caught up in emotional turbulence, close your eyes, focus on your Heart, let the breath flow gently—and bathe in the stillness and Love that is always available, emanating from your own Heart.

Ignore the drama: Vibrate higher.

LOVE MADE FLESH

All the ills of the world stem from the absence of Love. Anger, fear, greed, hatred, meanness, envy, antagonism and depression all come from the place where Love is not.

Lack of Love in a human being is like lack of sunlight for a plant. It causes something to shrivel and die, and the organism cannot be what it is meant to be.

When the necessary nourishment is not there, when there is a deficiency of one kind or another, the system does not function as it is meant to, and dysfunctional behavior of one sort or another manifests.

Love is the nutrient that provides peace and happiness. The necessary ingredient for self-confidence. Without Love there is no joy or even contentment. Success is not complete without Love, and neither fame nor fortune can take its place.

No matter how much one has or is or does, without Love there is a void that cannot be filled. A certain something, a restless longing: an empty place.

Love is experienced in, and emanates from, the Heart Center. *Each of us has the Source of Love within.*

You can know this by focusing your attention on that place and seeing or feeling it open up like a blooming flower. Close your eyes. Let the breath flow gently. Allow the sensation that arises to fill you, to wash over you. Bathe in it, be warmed and comforted by it.

And when you are filled to overflowing with that sweet sensation, send it out from your Heart to another. One you are close to, or a stranger in need. Send it to a place or people in distress. Send it to a world leader with more power than understanding or compassion. Send it out to encompass our precious planet—our Mother Earth—who is suffering mightily from our lack of Love and Loving-kindness.

By moving yourself into this state of Love, you are creating one more cell in the organism of this Creation which is healthy and whole. You are reversing the cancerous disease of unconscious existence that is eating it up alive. You are choosing Life and living over destruction and death. You are being who and what you are meant to be: Love made flesh—One.

LOVE, DEFINED

First understand this: Capital L Love is a frequency, not an emotion.

The fact that we have been programmed to believe that we are not complete without someone to love us (or even more insidiously, finding our so-called soul-mate) is the greatest deception and distraction of this modern era.

In fact, this concept—the necessity of having a partner in order to be 'in Love'—is responsible for the disconnect we experience with regard to our own Higher Selves, and interferes with our ability to experience ourselves as the Love we are in Truth.

We are One. All Life, is One. Everything that is, exists in one Unified Field. Within this Oneness each component, each being, vibrates at its own signature frequency. We are like the members of a choir, each carrying a different note, contributing to the hopefully pleasing sound of the whole. But unfortunately, unlike a choir, as humans we do not vibrate in harmony—barely being harmonious within our own selves— and so the result of our dissonant vibrational toning is cacophonous and chaotic, with the consequence being all the ills we experience as individuals and society as a whole.

✧ ✧ ✧

As individual cells in the body of humanity, if we want to enlighten that body and create a more Loving environment on the planet, each one of us must lighten up our own cell and contribute that Light to the whole.

And that's where Love comes in: Love is the highest frequency we achieve while in form and contains the greatest Light—why we often hear them linked together: Love & Light.

The frequency of Love emanates from the Heart-center—and if faithfully cultivated can be experienced directly as it begins to fill in all the cracks where fear, sadness or disconnection dwell. That Love-frequency transforms everything it touches, and it will transform you if you make it the focus of your attention.

"How do we do this?" you may ask.

One very simple yet powerful process is this: close your eyes, place your hands on your Heart center and repeat "I Love You" over and over and over. You can also look in the mirror and do the same thing. You can sing it in the shower or in the car while driving; you can repeat it when you're going to sleep and/or first thing upon awakening. I like to sing it and have created a jazzy little tune that feels delicious. (You can hear it in the Pecha Kucha video on my website: A Journey Into Love.)

One thing is for sure: if you do this simple little practice daily—and devotedly—in a very short period of time you will change the frequency in your body and energy field, begin to embody a higher vibration, and have an entirely transformed experience of yourself for starters, and Life on Earth in general. And that's when the real fun begins—because Joy arises in your Heart and you start to affect those around you by the Loving vibe you carry.

✧ ✧ ✧

For years now, as Valentine's Day approaches, I have been handing out hundreds of little reminders randomly on the street and in shops as I go about my day. Every year I choose a new graphic, but the message is always the same:

You ARE Love. Love yourself.

Take it to heart and see what happens.

I promise you:

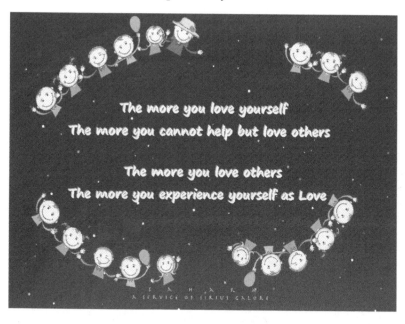

The more you love yourself
The more you cannot help but love others

The more you love others
The more you experience yourself as Love

LOVE, AGAIN

1—The more you love yourself, the more you experience yourself as Love.

2—The more you experience yourself as Love, the more you are deliberately Loving to others.

3—The more you are deliberately Loving to others—the more you experience yourself as Love—and, the more your personal energy field vibrates at a higher frequency.

4—The higher the frequency of your personal energy field—the more you experience yourself as Love—and, the more you are aligned with All-That-Is.

5—The more you are aligned with All-That-Is—the more you experience yourself as Love—and, the more the human aspect of Self dissolves into Love.

6—The more the human aspect of Self dissolves into Love—the more you experience yourself as Love—and, the more you choose to Uplift & Inspire.

7—The more you choose to Uplift & Inspire—the more you experience yourself as Love—and, (return to #2, *ad infinitum*).

Latest release from Cosmic Films Inc.

Love: A True Story

Playing everywhere

Find it in your own heart

SAHARA
A SERVICE OF SIRIUS GALORE

YOU CREATE YOUR OWN REALITY

What does it mean to "create your own reality"? It means, the *attitude* or *frequency of energy* you bring into your environment is going to be what appears in your life. The quality of energy you establish as your baseline is what determines your experience.

If I have cultivated the Love in my Heart, then when I get in my car and go out into the community, this is the quality of energy I am carrying and what I am going to experience: like attracts like.

But that's not the only thing going on: *The Universe is working with me to support my evolutionary process and encourage my highest potential.* So the Universe is going to send the *opposite* of the quality I have been cultivating as an opportunity for me to experience and *demonstrate* where I'm at: am I firmly fixed in Heart-centered Consciousness or do I need more practice?

If I'm firmly fixed and something unloving shows up in my world, I'm going to respond with Love. Love is my ground, Love is where I live, Love is what I am and all it is possible for me to express.

If, occasionally, I find myself reacting in a way less than Loving, it's obvious. Then, a realization arises and an auto-correction takes place, and the persona adjusts for the new data.

This is how I've "created my own reality"—by choosing to hold and generate a certain frequency of energy from moment to moment. I then find myself in a world where Love, Compassion and Kindness reign and Goodness is the prevailing atmosphere.

❖ ❖ ❖

There's another component as well: where do I put my attention? If I pay attention to that which disturbs me, I'll be disturbed. If I pay attention to that which inspires, encourages, delights me—I'll be inspired, encouraged and delighted.

If your world is less than Loving, take a good look at yourself and see what frequency of energy you are cultivating and generating in your life, and where you are putting your attention.

And while we cannot control what arises around us, *we have the ability to choose how we respond* to what arises, and, we get to choose where we direct our attention and what we support 'out there' with our energy.

❖ ❖ ❖

And we must be very careful not to succumb to the blame-game—the preeminent tool of the divide-and-conquer contingent. Each one of us is playing the role we came here to play in this very sophisticated movie called: Life On Earth. If you can be convinced that someone is to blame (in your personal life or in the public sector), regardless of the descriptors that can be applied to that personality—if your attention can be continuously diverted to someone/something outside yourself—then you may neglect to look at your own part: how *you* behave/think/speak—and you won't be taking responsibility for how *you* could change to be a more Loving contribution to the whole.

❖ ❖ ❖

I'm sure you've heard the expression: Where attention goes, energy flows. Thus, we create our own reality and get to dwell in it. You actually have the power to create your own Heaven or Hell right here on Earth.

Now what are you going to do???

NOT MY CIRCUS, NOT MY MONKEYS

We each live in our own world—a world we have created by our attitude, desire, choice, attention and intention.

In my world, Love, Kindness, Peace & Harmony reign.

This world supports me, and this reality inspires me.

I live in this reality by my own choosing, by my own intention. I live in this reality by focusing my attention on all that is good, uplifting, inspiring—on the Love that I am and the Love that I perceive all around me; on the Light that I know myself to be, and the Light that I see in others.

And the more I cultivate that Love and Light within me, the more I see it around me. It increases daily—and I receive the benefit: it's a closed circuit, nourishing itself. I thrive.

At the same time, by choosing Love as my baseline, I infuse its qualities into the environment around me, and share these qualities with those in that environment—uplifting and inspiring others by the energies I embody, by my speaking and behavior. I am doing my part in "transforming the fabric of reality for the well-being of all" to the best of my ability.

And all around me, wherever I look, I see the world transforming: I see caring and kindness, progress in sustainability, improvement in quality of life. I see education that nourishes the being, the choosing of people over profit. I see humor, I see Consciousness, I see equality expanding—I see a new world dawning.

But I also see those attached to and invested in the energies of the Old Paradigm contorted with excruciating madness, while it goes through its death throes. Their antics are absurd and appalling at the same time, but serve a purpose in the greater scheme of things: ripping away the veil of illusion with a vengeance and inspiring those with goodness in their Hearts out of complacency and into action.

And while I may be aware of its existence, I don't dwell on the madness—it will run its course and expire.

I choose instead to feed my energy into my preferred reality—for that is where it serves in the highest capacity.

I have no interest in fighting against—I prefer to nurture, to support, to inspire.

You may call me deluded, "You may say that I'm a dreamer—but I'm not the only one…"

YOU ARE NOT WHAT YOU THINK

This can be read in two ways:

You are not what you think, meaning: the thoughts you have about your identity are inaccurate, and

You are not what you think, meaning: you, are not your thoughts.

Who do you think you are?

To what extent do you identify with:

Your physical body, the voice in your head, your personality, nationality, beliefs?

Can you acknowledge to what extent you have been programmed by the society you live in regarding how you view the world and perceive yourself?

Do you think you're limited by the amount of money in your pocket or bank account?

✧ ✧ ✧

Take a journey with me—read the following to the end, get a sense of what I'm saying, then close your eyes and go through the process:

Be still.

Place yourself in a desert: no flora, no fauna, blue sky, mild temperature, seated comfortably.

Strip off your jewelry, take off your watch, remove your makeup, shed your clothes.

Imagine that you have no hair.

Forget about your job, your family, your home, your wealth or lack.

Wipe out all memory of the past.

Withdraw your attention from the body.

Thoughts cease.

Eyes see the vast expanse without judgment.

Only Awareness is. Feel it.

SELF-OBSERVATION IS THE KEY

Self-observation ultimately resides in the Awareness that exists independent of the organism—an Awareness that enables a perception other than the everyday Pavlovian response to sensory, mental, environmental and societal input. But at the onset, one must begin to *pay attention*.

In the previous handbook I introduced the three little steps that set you on the road to self-mastery: mastering the auto-responses of the unenlightened self.

The three aspects of human function that require observation—so that we may rise above our conditioning and move into conscious mastery—are:

Thought, speaking and behavior.

I'll reiterate the first one here (you may extrapolate on speaking and behavior) as it is the key to everything, and where you'll have to begin if you would free yourself from society's programming: the programming that exists to make you part of its economic machine, serving its purpose with no care for your personal existence.

❖ ❖ ❖

There are two types of thoughts:

There are the thoughts that arise, and have been shown by science to activate the brain (and the thinking process) before we become aware of them,* and,

there are the thoughts we intentionally think when we are engaged in a practical endeavor: planning a meal or a trip; conjuring a garden or design for a bed-frame.

The second: practical, consciously evoked thoughts, we need not bother with—they are concerned with useful action.

The first, those thoughts that arise, unbidden, out of our subconscious soup, are the ones that create the mischief and must be reckoned with in order for us to achieve self-mastery and peace of mind.

❖ ❖ ❖

In order to free ourselves from the subjugation of the thoughts that arise, we must first begin to *pay attention*.

This means, that as a thought arises one is not (in the usual way) automatically hooked into it—carried along that trajectory willy-nilly—but one notices it in the same way one may notice a cloud in a clear sky, or horns honking as cars pass. Then, with awareness, one chooses whether that thought is desirable for engagement or not, and then proceeds *to engage consciously* or dismiss, as desired.

If, for example, the thought is a reminder of something that needs doing, we engage and move into deliberate thinking and/or action regarding the subject, or make a note to remind us that something needs to be done.

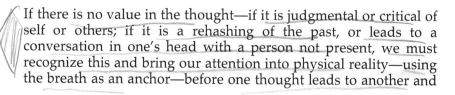

If there is no value in the thought—if it is judgmental or critical of self or others; if it is a rehashing of the past, or leads to a conversation in one's head with a person not present, we must recognize this and bring our attention into physical reality—using the breath as an anchor—before one thought leads to another and we are led into a fantasy-world of agitation, grief and/or depression, distracted from what-is and stuck in an imaginary story that takes us nowhere.

The inability to master the thoughts that arise is the basis of all suffering. So start paying attention and become the master of self you are meant to be.

*See: Free Will/Sam Harris, neuroscientist. A short, easy-to-read discourse on the neuroscience of thought and behavior.

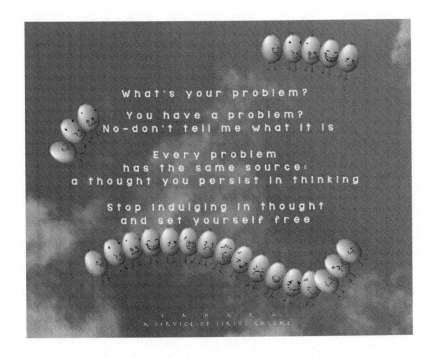

*Unwavering identification
with personality and its attributes
is a sure-fire means
of deterring
expansion of Consciousness*

AWARENESS

Self-observation leads to Awareness

Awareness promotes clarity

Clarity invites intention

Intention precipitates conscious, higher choices

Conscious, higher choices elevate frequency

Higher frequency fosters elevated Consciousness

To begin, we must first cultivate the awareness of the Awareness that is always present. This may be experienced by sitting quietly, eyes open, feeling the breath moving into and out of the body, and simply observing the sensations within the body and whatever exists in the environment. By not labeling anything we see, the sense of just-being arises. And present in that beingness is Awareness.

This Awareness is an attribute of the Higher Self, of which the human portion is the smallest, densest part. You may imagine the human to be a projection of this Higher Self, which in turn may be imagined as a large energy- or Light-body.

At the beginning of my awareness of Awareness, I experienced its presence just behind the right side of my head. I was perceiving through my eyes and from this out-of-body perspective at the same time. The out-of-body Awareness added a detached perception to what I was seeing around me and simultaneously, a perception of what was going on inside: the thoughts arising, the emotional responses, and the sensations in my body.

This enabled me to recognize that I was considerably more than the body, and not confined by or to it: to begin to perceive myself in an expansive, formless way, and not as a small, limited, mortal human.

After some time of paying attention to that Awareness, that out-of-body perspective merged into the looking-out-of-my-eyes perception, and from that time forward became integrated into my walking-around state. This is what will happen in you if you apply yourself to the practice. You can call it: expanded, or integrated, Consciousness.

If you can maintain an awareness of the thoughts as they arise, of the words as they leave your mouth, of the actions as they occur, you will begin to experience yourself as Consciousness in connection to the organism—rather than being trapped within the body and able to perceive/experience only with/through the senses, colored by the so-called mind.

This creates the expansion and distance that enables the Higher Self to establish a clearer connection with the organism, becoming the driver of the vehicle in its Higher purpose, and liberating the character from the emotional and psychological discomfort of its imaginary identity.

What a relief!

How I respond
is what demonstrates
how Aware I am

And how Aware I am
is what determines
how I respond

S   A   H   A   R   A
A SERVICE OF SIRIUS GALORE

FREQUENCY

Capital A Awareness and frequency are inextricably linked: Awareness elevates frequency and frequency determines the degree of Awareness.

Since we are energy transmitters and receivers, whatever frequency or quality of energy we transmit or express, that is the frequency or quality of energy we attract, receive, and experience.

Once we have become aware of our greater Selves, we have the ability to cultivate higher frequencies in our energy field in numerous ways, having to do with our choices of input and output.

Input may be designated as the quality or vibration of energy we consume through our senses and otherwise: the company we keep; the media we watch, read, or listen to; the environment we dwell in; food, drink, and drugs; the events in which we engage; and especially, the Love we intentionally activate and cultivate.

Output may be defined as the thoughts we think; the way we speak and what we say; attitude and attributes of character; the way we conduct ourselves in relationships, encounters; and our way of being in society-at-large.

For instance, as previously mentioned, if our speaking often dwells on complaint, criticism and judgment, we are creating a miasma of low frequency energy in our body and field, with the potential consequences of physical, mental and/or psychological illness and myriad undesirable circumstances.

By making choices and changes in all the above, frequency is affected and elevated, and as frequency is elevated there is more room for the presence of Consciousness to establish itself in the organism, more of one's Higher Self is embodied, and one is less at-effect-of one's human foibles—which become a source of amusement and insight.

The higher the frequency we embody, the more we are aligned with Source, the greater our capacity for Service, and the more satisfying and de-Light-ful our lives.

Step up.

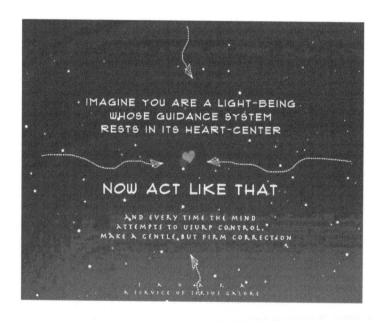

FREQUENCY, TAKE 2

Everything is energy—and energy vibrates at different frequencies.

When we come into this world, most of us are vibrating at a frequency much closer to the Divine than the human. Depending on the family/circumstances we are born into—and the subsequent environment and programming we are subjected to—we are often, gradually, conditioned to the lower common denominator of human society.

Also, because of this exposure to collective consciousness and its effects, and because of the personal storyline of trauma/drama we live through—we come to believe we are the characters we find ourselves playing, and we identify with the attributes of those characters, for good or ill.

Thus we experience the emotional and psychological disturbances that result from the misidentification with the human aspect of our beings.

✧ ✧ ✧

To reiterate: Everything is energy—and energy vibrates at different frequencies.

Now, as humans, once a certain degree of awakening has occurred, we have the ability to make *conscious* choice, and with this ability to choose we have the capacity to lift ourselves out of the maelstrom that is 3D reality, and into a more refined existence where the Love frequency is the default vibration.

This doesn't necessarily mean that the physical circumstances change, though they may—it means that, because we are vibrating at a higher frequency, **we** change in a way that creates a new perception of what-is, and thus our experience of what-is is completely different. Once that happens, everything can change— but it's effortless.

It may not be an easy journey, because one is overcoming the habits of a lifetime, but the dedication necessary brings multiple rewards—the greatest being relief from suffering.

Now before you get the wrong idea, let's define suffering as used in this context:

It is not deprivation, not physical pain, not abuse. All of these are circumstance.

Suffering is a mental condition that develops from our engagement with and indulgence in the thoughts that arise, and *the stories we then tell ourselves about our circumstances.* This then becomes a vicious circle and self-fulfilling prophecy.

If we want to raise our frequency, and begin to align with our own Higher, more Divine Selves—our birthright—we must begin with self-observation: how we speak and what we say; how we behave and what we do; and the basis of it all—how we choose to engage with the thoughts that arise.

In order to do this the most vital activity is <u>paying attention</u>, **being aware of the thoughts as they arise**, and then mastering the ability to choose which thoughts are worthy of engagement, and which thoughts will lead us down the rabbit hole to a hell of our own devising.

If you want out of your suffering—pay attention, and choose wisely.

*What if
you stopped thinking of yourself
as a person*

*and started thinking of yourself
as a Spirit-Being,
using the body to fulfill the role
you came here to play?*

FREE WILL

If you think/believe you have free will, then the greatest use you can make of it is choosing how you want to **be** in each moment.

You can say what you like about free will and manifestation. To me, free will has more to do with attitude than the ability to make something happen.

For in the same way that laboratory rats are subjected to stimuli, and run through their mazes to find the object of their desire— food, sex, domination/survival—until a higher level of Consciousness is attained, humankind also mostly functions in response to stimuli: biological, environmental, psychological, emotional, societal.

In my experience, I have been guided, driven, carried, inspired and supported—and the only thing I can take credit for is a yearning heart and the determination to know and integrate the Light I Am.

I don't feel that I have earned anything I possess—everything I have has been given to me.

If you want to spend your life trying to manifest the things of this world, be my guest. But aligning yourself with the Source of everything will fulfill the dreams you didn't even know you had.

Yet what if we accept the premise that free-will, as commonly conceived, is so? In that case, you get to choose whatever you please.

What if you choose to apply your free-will to how you show up, how you respond, how you feel about yourself, how you treat others, how/what you think, how you speak?

Do you actually have the capacity to do that? Then be my guest: exercise your free-will, *choose* who/how you want to be and show me who you are.

If you consider yourself to be on the spiritual path, or consciously working on expansion of Consciousness, or not, observe yourself:

See how reactive you are to what goes on around you.

How at-effect you are of your environment and circumstances.

If you think you are master of your world, then master yourself. See if you can stop reacting automatically to the stimuli around you. See if you can tap into the Love that you are, and remain there unmoved, regardless.

Watch how you show up in front of others, and see if you have the ability to exercise your free-will and choose Love over irritation, Love over anger, Love over fear. Observe how much you criticize, condemn, complain and pass judgment. These attitudes are the antithesis of Love. See how much you refuse to accept, how much you resist what-is.

Observe yourself and discover to what extent you are actually in control of what you consider 'your' life.

Please—utilize your free-will.

'MANIFESTATION'

What's the point of manifestation if after you've obtained whatever it is you think you want, the one you think you are is still there, dissatisfied?

If you are intrigued by the idea of manifestation, why don't you manifest a quiet mind? Why don't you manifest serenity? Why don't you manifest a Loving Heart? Abounding Joy?

It's not a question of obtaining—objects, achievements, relationships, wealth or acclaim—or of arranging your world in a manner that you imagine will create the most comfortable environment or circumstance.

It's a question of letting go of what you consider to be the personal identity that you cling to regardless of the suffering it brings you.

The current very trendy idea of manifestation is simply another distraction that embroils you in the personal, keeping you engaged in desire and preventing you from relaxing into and dwelling in your True Nature.

If you imagine you are a someone—whatever the vicissitudes of that someone's life, for good or ill—all the energetic roiling of life-on-earth is going to be experienced as waves of disturbance in the body and being, tossing about that someone as if on a stormy sea.

However, if the 'you' you think you are is able to dissolve into the expansive Awareness you are in Truth, that elevated state perceives those waves as if from great heights—where they are of no more consequence than a microbe is to the someone.

Pleasure and pain may still be experienced, but one is no longer striving for the one and shrinking from the other.

Peace reigns. Love is. Suffering ends.

Still want to manifest?

Fully embodied Consciousness—manifest that.

EFFORTLESS LIVING:
RUNNING ON AUTOPILOT

Every true artist of whatever medium, and every genius, too, will acknowledge that inspiration comes *to* them, and their art or brilliance is something that comes *through them* and not from them.

And this is also what happens when a certain frequency is attained in one's energy field—one has moved into a particular slipstream of Consciousness and is in attunement/alignment with the Intelligence that enables them to be the conduit for whatever wants to manifest through them.

Einstein referred to it, Tesla acknowledged it, and any true artist of any stripe will admit it: at our best, we are conduits through which the energy of Infinite Intelligence flows, bringing what It will.

But in order to move into that slipstream, one must first have an inkling of one's True Identity: the *original* identity having nothing to do with the body, economic status, intellectual achievement, relationships, national or religious associations, name, fame, etc.

And for each one of us that original identity is the same: *an entirely unique and individualized aspect of the singular Cosmic Is-ness*—Consciousness in form.

✧ ✧ ✧

When we recognize and choose to align with Consciousness Itself, we get switched on, as it were, and begin living and serving in the capacity in which we are meant to live and serve.

Life becomes effortless.

We live on autopilot: being inspired, following direction, playing our role, serving our purpose—and experiencing the greatest satisfaction possible as a human being.

But until that higher frequency is locked-in, the organism remains driven by the un-mastered thoughts that arise—and the unchecked reactivity of the mind and senses is what runs the show.

Self-mastery in relation to thought is the kindergarten of Higher Consciousness—as all human suffering begins with being at-effect-of the thoughts that arise—and liberation commences by mastering one's response to those thoughts.

Once that happens, a higher frequency can be established in the energy field, and alignment with All-That-Is can occur.

There is nothing sweeter than giving up the imaginary reins we think we hold, and allowing Infinite Intelligence—via our own Higher Self—to take over and run the story. Wonder and miracles abound, synchronicity is the norm, and life becomes magical.

And the greatest benefit for a human character is: the more we move into that slipstream of Grace, the less suffering we have to endure.

❖ ❖ ❖

There are a lots of teachers making lots of money encouraging you to hold those reins and steer your life where you will.

I am encouraging the opposite—and giving it to you right here: let go, recognize and align with your Highest Self, and begin to enjoy the life you are meant to live—effortlessly.

DEALING WITH IT

I am not immune to unpleasant thoughts that arise—they are part of human existence.

The difference is how I deal with them.

First of all, I've trained myself to notice the thoughts AS THEY ARISE, so I am not in an auto-reactive state. (This is the most valuable tool one can possess if one is interested in intentional participation in one's evolutionary process.) Since this is so, I get to choose if I want to engage with that thought or not.

For the most part, if the thought is not of a practical nature (remember to fill the gas tank) I give it a flick and direct my attention to what-is in physical reality, but occasionally something comes up that triggers a vestige of emotional detritus hanging around in the subconscious and the personal energy field.

When this occurs, I recognize the need for energetic house-cleaning and let it rip. This means I allow the energy to move through me as it will, which may include focusing on the breath, vocalizing, tears, body movement or whatever else presents itself.

The experience can be compared to being caught in a strong wave at the beach: one is tumbled about underwater for whatever period of time it takes for that wave (read: energy) to dissipate on the shore, and then one is tossed up and able to breathe again. With the proper understanding of what's happening, we allow ourselves to surrender to the power of that wave, as attempting to fight it is like beating yourself up while being beaten up.

The emotional or psychic energy that was stuck in the energy field then rips its way out and—after a period of gentle breathing and perhaps a drink of water—equanimity is restored, Consciousness is present, and I haven't told myself any stories based on the thought or the ensuing sensations in the body. I've simply eliminated what could be compared to a virus interfering with my default programming, and emerged into a more aligned position with the Light I Am.

If I can do it, you can do it too.

Note: I can also recommend the Energy Transfer process offered *gratis* online by Ethann Fox, as a means of clearing emotional and / or psychological static out of one's field and body.

ON 'DEPRESSION'

Note: this piece was written because I noticed posts on fb about people being 'depressed.' Unless you've got a chemical imbalance in your brain, your so-called depression is the result of uncontrolled indulgence in the thoughts that arise in your head, period. (See graphic at "Self-observation is the Key")

EVERYONE has had challenges, some that are not always obvious. There are those without sight, without limbs, with biological or neurological aberrations that create hardships others cannot imagine; those who do not fit into what society considers the norm and are reviled, attacked or ostracized. No one can say: "My pain is greater than your pain—I'm the pain champion, acknowledge me."

In 74 years in this body, my experience has been riddled with loss, grief, cruelty, unimaginable challenge, deprivation, limitation, emotional pain—blah, blah, blah.

And—I understand that whatever shows up in life happens not **to** us, but **for** us—because we are beings meant to evolve in Consciousness, to own our status as aspects of the Source, and to know ourselves as individual sparks of Light in the Quantum Field of existence.

Despite all the hardships, the adversity, the struggle—I've never considered myself a victim—not even of the 'non-consensual sex' I experienced as a teenager. I've chewed it up and spit it out, turning it into compost to nurture the fruit that wanted to grow on my tree.

I've taken everything life has thrown at me and used it like a chisel to chip away all that is extraneous to the Consciousness waiting to be revealed in each of us—like the beauty of a statue hidden in a block of marble. With the mountain of lemons life has handed me, I've made a lemon meringue pie so rich and delicious, that like the loaves and the fishes, it's available to feed all those who are hungry.

And if I can do it, you can do it, too.

We are NEVER victims—helpless creatures of circumstance, of biology, of the behavior of others. We contain within us the Power of Love, the same power that created the Universe itself and this beautiful planet that we have the privilege to inhabit—and with that power we can choose *how we respond* to what life gives us. We can choose to be resentful of, broken and defeated by, our circumstances—or to use those circumstances to become masters of the self that nothing can hurt, nothing can offend, nothing can insult, nothing can defeat.

Note: Actually, there IS a time when we are victims: WHEN WE MAKE OURSELVES VICTIMS BY THE THOUGHTS WE THINK about ourselves or about what has occurred. We victimize ourselves with self-criticism and self-judgment. We victimize ourselves by imagining we are at-effect-of what others may have 'done to us.' Being at-effect-of is a choice. When we understand that what others do or say is about them and not us—AND that everyone is doing the best they can given *their* back-story—we achieve a certain level of awareness (and emotional maturity) and then we move out of victimhood into self-mastery.

ANGELS AWAKENING—
AA OF THE NEW PARADIGM

I used to have a friend in Alcoholics Anonymous. One time I asked him: How can you hope to change your patterns of behavior if 5 to 7x a week in a meeting you affirm: "My name is ____, and I'm an alcoholic.?"

At the time, I suggested, (if he had the nerve to buck the system), why don't you state instead: "My name is ____, and I am a child of God, an expression of All-That-Is."

That thought inspired the conceptual Angels Awakening—AA of the New Paradigm:

As part of the Great Transformation, untold numbers of souls have felt the need for a support system.

To meet that need, Angels Awakening (AA) has been created.

If you'd like to be part of this group repeat after me:

"My name is _____and I am a Being of Light. I am awakening to my True Identity, and I am ready to participate in transforming the fabric of reality for the well-being of all."

There are only 3 steps:

1- ADMIT that there is a Higher Power, and that *It has manifested as the unique expression of Infinite Intelligence that you are,* in order to experience and celebrate Itself as you, and participate in "transforming the fabric of reality for the well-being of all."

2- ACCEPT that as a unique expression *of* Source you have the ability to experience yourself *as* Source and *choose* to participate in "transforming the fabric of reality for the well-being of all."

3- ACKNOWLEDGE that the Source of Love and all you desire resides within your own Heart, and choose to connect with That— so you may participate in "transforming the fabric of reality for the well-being of all."

You may notice the repetition of a certain phrase: "transforming the fabric of reality for the well-being of all." For many on the planet at this time, it's the reason we're here.

It is this intention we are being called to embrace and embody—to release the personal desires of the persona and step into an amalgamation of Energy forming on the planet in the guise of humans living ordinary lives and doing ordinary things, but carrying a high frequency of Light in their bodies and beings as a contribution to the transformation that wishes to manifest in the world.

Angels are awakening all around the world—welcome to the New Paradigm.

LIVIN' LARGE—IT'S NOT WHAT YOU THINK

The mindset of American society would have us believe that unless one is possessed of name and fame, pots of money, and a lavish lifestyle, one cannot be said to be livin' large.

Ironically that's not the case. For while social media and ubiquitous selfies give us the impression of popularity amongst an online audience, and we're convinced that having thousands of so-called friends and likes give us recognition and status—in fact, an individual of any economic stratum is living a small life if the primary focus of their time, energy, and attention is the mere satisfaction of their own personal needs and desires.

To live large, one must needs live as a conscious and cognizant element of and contributor to the Quantum Field that consists of everything and everyone, and may be seen to operate as a single organism when one looks beyond the apparent and discovers the greater Reality.

To truly live large, one must understand our Oneness, go beyond the personal, and live a life consciously contributing to "transforming the fabric of reality for the well-being of all."

Wanna live large? Go for it!

Cultivate ~ Embody ~ Circulate

Love

SAHARA
A SERVICE OF SIRIUS GALORE

YOUR JOB AND YOU

You think your work is XYZ or finding a way to make $$ and 'support' yourself. It's not.

Your essential work at this point in time is to cultivate Consciousness and bloom.

We do this by generating as much Love and kindness as possible in our daily encounters, which serves to increase the frequency of our energy-body. The higher the frequency of our energy field, the more Light we contain—and the greater the Consciousness available.

As we attain higher and higher levels of Consciousness, the less we have to consider the 'how' of living—as it becomes a Grace-full flow of synchronicity.

So whatever 'job' you've been given (or chosen) to do or whatever role you've been given (or chosen) to play, that is simply how you are occupying your time—the most superficial function.

The hidden, esoteric, Cosmic purpose of your being in that location with those people is to bring as much Light into that environment as possible—by being kind, patient, considerate, cooperative, good-natured, supportive and Loving—demonstrating what it is to be a ideal human being.

If you'd like to accelerate The Great Transformation,* alleviate the suffering of our brothers and sisters around the world, and create Heaven on Earth, please—do your job.

*The Great Transformation is what I am calling the current period of societal upheaval (and dissolution of the old paradigm) that is precipitating profound change on the planet. And now, with the appearance of Covid, we are in the midst of the greatest transformation the world has ever seen. Out of the wildfire of insanity ignited by madmen, the Phoenix of Consciousness is arising.

REGARDING 'ASCENSION'

(A phrase being bandied about in certain spiritual circles)

Let those with the ears to hear, hear:

You are not your body.

Your body is a vehicle for the Consciousness you are, existing for the purpose of Service to the planet on which you dwell.

While you remain under the illusion of believing yourself to be the body/persona and its myriad attributes, you suffer all the ills associated with human emotion and psychology.

Once you liberate yourself from that limiting belief, you begin the process you call Ascension, which is actually an **integration** of the Consciousness you are with the body it inhabits: more and more of the Consciousness is present in the body, while the frequency of the body is refined to harmonize with the Consciousness.

This so-called Ascension is actually an elevation of frequency in your energy field that enables you have a more refined experience, being less at-effect-of the density that exists in 3-D and able to live "in the world while not being of it."

✧ ✧ ✧

It's a challenging process, as the 3-D world is engaging and distracting to the persona in the same way a theme park is engaging and distracting to a child: it engages the senses and emotions—powerful forces of distraction indeed.

But by knowing yourself as Consciousness—not in an intellectual way, but by direct perception—and then acting *as* Consciousness, you begin to anchor that frequency into your energy field, and find yourself dwelling in a parallel reality, even though you still perceive the 3D world.

In that parallel reality, the density of the world you inhabit (the emotional and psychological attachments and their effects) slowly dissolves, as all that static exists at a lower frequency than the one you now embody.

Then, as you are relieved of that density, experiencing yourself lighter and Lighter, you are in a greater position to fulfill the role you came to play: "transforming the fabric of reality for the well-being of all"—and, because you have positioned yourself as a conscious contributor to the well-being of all, you are supported in ways both material and profound.

Get on board—it's the ride of a lifetime.

Promote Love

Cultivate Loving Energy
Embody A Loving Frequency
Think Loving Thoughts
Speak Loving Words
Do Loving Deeds
Embrace Loving Ideas
Express Loving Attitudes

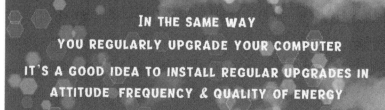

IN THE SAME WAY
YOU REGULARLY UPGRADE YOUR COMPUTER
IT'S A GOOD IDEA TO INSTALL REGULAR UPGRADES IN
ATTITUDE FREQUENCY & QUALITY OF ENERGY

SAHARA
A SERVICE OF SIRIUS GALORE

FREQUENCY CHANGES EVERYTHING— LET'S SWITCH TIMELINES

Change yourself & change the world

You may think we are doomed to the looming climate change catastrophe, which would be dire indeed, but while the timeline in play at this moment definitely seems to be leading in the direction of a perilously devastated world—**we**, collectively, have the power to shift timelines, avert catastrophe, and create a happy ending. Not only in terms of our precious biosphere—but equally as important, in terms of the 'sociosphere,' which term I am using to indicate the condition of humanity and its societies.

Despite Greta Thunberg and her heroic efforts in challenging world governments and activating her generation, we know that governments and legislation cannot be relied upon to make the changes necessary *in a timely manner*. **We** have to act now, and we have to power to do so.

When I say "Ignore the Drama—Vibrate Higher" I am suggesting, requesting, encouraging, and beseeching you to understand that you have the ability—and the responsibility—to "change yourself & change the world."

How? Well may you ask.

Everything is energy, energy vibrates at different frequencies, and depending on the frequency in play we have Love, Joy, and Harmony—or fear, aggression, chaos and devastation.

Right now, on the surface, the collective frequency is exhibiting the effects of the latter—but what most cannot perceive is the groundswell of the former, precipitated by individuals worldwide who have lifted themselves out of the 3D static and have ascended *energetically* to a Higher Consciousness and Higher Reality.

The fact is, humans around the world are waking up, recognizing themselves as Light Beings in a human body, and cultivating a higher frequency in their personal energy fields, which in turn is contributing more Light to the Quantum Field and resulting in movement toward a kinder, gentler humanity.*

(In case you don't know: the Quantum Field—finally discovered and confirmed by science—is the energetic field in which we play and contains everything and everyone. Knowingly or unknowingly, we all contribute to it and are all affected by it. As conscious beings, we also have our own electro-magnetic field, and a personal frequency signature. We operate as transmitting/receiving stations: picking up signals from hither and yon, and constantly broadcasting signals based on the state of our energy field in any given moment: either emotional/mental static, or the harmony/serenity inherent in functioning as Consciousness itself.)

You have the choice—and responsibility—right now: exactly how you'd like to position yourself in terms of the quality of your contribution. Because it's already happening either consciously or unconsciously, and simply calling yourself spiritual doesn't cut it if you haven't activated and embodied the Love you are, and developed sufficient self-mastery to affect the frequency you hold and emanate.

If you haven't mastered your reactions to the thoughts that arise, if you haven't mastered your speaking (in terms of intention, integrity and follow-through), if you haven't integrated Awareness in your actions, you are something of a pinball: bounced around willy-nilly, at-effect-of random societal or internal input, and subject to all the emotional and psychological static inherent in the 3rd dimension: Life on Earth as a mostly reactive human.

However, once you **choose** to activate and enhance the Love-frequency in your energy field, and cultivate the Awareness necessary to become a master of thought, word and deed, you lift yourself out of that 3rd dimensional chaos and into a realm where Harmony reigns.

You have upgraded the frequency in your energy field, you are in closer alignment with the Light Being you are, and life becomes increasingly effortless as your trajectory continues on an upward path.

You are not only in sync with the Legions of Light that are doing everything in their power to uplift and inspire humanity in its transition, you are a making a definitive contribution in the focused endeavor to "transform the fabric of reality for the well-being of all."

And that, my dears, is what we came here to do.

*Jeremy Rifkin's *Homo Empathicus*

The greatest thing you can do

for your self & for the planet

is cease to identify as the character

you are playing

and realize that

you are an embodiment of

Love & Light

I've been inspired to start a pyramid scheme, and I invite you all to participate.

It's the well-known scheme in reverse: instead of the one at the top profiting hugely from all the suckers who are convinced they will get-rich-quick—the one at the top is the perpetual giver, and each successive level, receiving the benefit of that initial giving, allows that wave of energetic giving to flow through them, giving freely.

Here's how it works: I'm the giver at the top of the pyramid— open to and constantly receiving from Source—and everyone is welcome to come to me and receive what I have to give.

My job is to Uplift & Inspire, upgrade your frequency, and assist you in fulfilling the role you are here to play.

If you choose to receive, you become a giver, too, giving whatever it is *you* have to offer.

(As the current economic system is still in place, this will have to be done extra-curricularly as it were—I'm not asking you to give up your day job. But that doesn't mean you can't choose to give your (fill-in-the-blank) to someone in need who may not be able to afford the cost.)

Once you've established yourself in this process (as an open channel), and your giving flows freely from your Heart, you will notice what may be called the 'stardust-effect'—unexpected blessings showing up, or the lights all turning green as you drive through town—little or not so little occurrences that make you sit up and take notice: the Universe smiling on you.

Since this is not a profit-based system but a Cosmic playground, you needn't join my pyramid—you can start one of your own with whatever it is you have to give, and invite those in your community to receive from you.

By establishing yourself as a perpetual giver, whether or not you are receiving from me, or creating a giving-pyramid of your own, you are placing yourself in a position for benevolent Cosmic energies to flow into and through you. Doesn't that sound lovely?

Now here's your invitation:
I'm available—come and get it.

LET'S BE CLEAR

What is my purpose in promoting the Evolution Revolution or the Great Transformation?

To contribute to the metamorphosis of our precious Planet from a place of conflict and greed, to a world where care and nurturance of the ecosystem itself and all its inhabitants is the Prime Directive.

To facilitate the creation of societies everywhere in which Consciousness informs the use of technology, and technology serves humanity and not vice versa.

To inspire the understanding: We are One & there's enough, and, Whatsoever we do to or for another, we are doing to or for our own selves.

I have no interest in amassing followers or making money from you by creating product or seminars. I just want you to get the message, integrate it into your life, and embody it in your daily living—thereby contributing to the aforementioned transformation and the Well-being of All.

Especially at this time—if you're not consciously part of the solution, you are unconsciously part of the problem.

With Great Love,
Sahara

YOU
ARE THE
LIGHT
OF THE WORLD
TURN YOURSELF ON
S A H A R A
A SERVICE OF SIRIUS GALORE

ADDENDA

A LITTLE BACKGROUND

Who Cares? Compassion in the 21st Century

In 1994 I was struck homeless in the same way Ramdass/Richard Alpert considers he was 'stroked'—by an intangible force. One day I was relocating from a northern state to a more desirable clime, a week later I was sleeping in my car, realizing my life would never be the same.

Nothing and everything in the previous forty-seven years of my existence had prepared me for the experience that ensued. And while I recognized the spiritual aspect of what was happening, that knowledge didn't ameliorate the harshness of the consequences, and I often wondered what I had done to deserve such a fate. My experience since then has demonstrated quite clearly that we do not have the control we think we have over our destiny, and begs the question "What is it that actually moves us through this life?"

The query often posed by well-meaning acquaintances, "Why don't you just get a job?" could not be answered. I knew that this situation was not about 'getting a job'—it was both a testing and an education: quite an extraordinary education in acceptance, non-judgment, trust and compassion—a curriculum unfortunately not available in our institutions of academe.

I learned, for instance, that however much there was, there was always enough to share—that the amount of food I thought I needed to satisfy my own hunger, when divided to provide sustenance for another, was somehow able to satisfy the hunger of both. Perhaps the act of sharing magically intensified the qualitative value of the food, or perhaps by sharing we precipitate Love. Lovers, as everyone knows, can live on air.

The friendships I made supported me and the kindness of strangers sustained me. I was particularly astonished by the deli manager in a supermarket who, when I'd have only thirty-two cents or some equally paltry amount to my name and request that amount of a particular foodstuff, would then give me a huge portion of that item and proceed to ring up whatever the amount I had mentioned. And I will never forget one fellow in a similar boat to mine who, when once I asked if he could spare a couple of dollars for lunch, took out and looked at the five singles his wallet contained and proceeded to give me *three* of them.

If we understand that humans are not only expressions *of* but conduits *for* the Divine, we understand that although fear might attempt to tell us otherwise, we are not limited by what we either possess or lack. After all, a tree produces more branches when pruned, and a plant more flowers when they are picked.

So if you consider yourself among the evolutionally advanced, walk the talk. "Think globally, act locally" is not just a catchy phrase.

Be an open channel for the energy of compassion to flow though you—on its way it will enhance the Love in your heart and create moments of wonder and awe at events which arise.

Be non-judgmental. *If we take the position that need exists in some to awaken compassion in others and open our hearts, we will be the ones who benefit the most.*

Trust me on this—I am speaking from experience.

For the past twelve years of 'homelessness' I have been the witness to, recipient of and instrument in acts of wonder and mystery that defy explanation. Over and over *and over* the trust I was drilled in proved itself profoundly, with the situations occurring and bounty extended ofttimes overwhelming in their breadth and depth of wonder-fullness.

And while I don't expect anyone else to willingly embrace the deprivation and suffering I have endured on my own journey—not a position one may volunteer for at any rate—I can honestly say that I don't regret a moment and have been transformed in ways both simple and profound.

The fact is, whether our lives are a series of cause and effect events or simply a storyline we meander through, the outcome is the same. And whether we are able to manipulate or cajole others to achieve our ends is always a crapshoot. The upshot being: when we lie on our deathbeds what will have been our greatest achievement—the things we have accumulated or the hearts we have touched?

One road leaves us tragically empty, the other filled in an incomparable way. I know the acts of kindness shown me have been light years more meaningful than all the expensive stuff I've acquired that has slipped through my fingers like grains of sand.

If we are not evolving into a civilization that understands and meets the needs of *all* its members as any enlightened family does, we are degenerating into a civilization that is self-righteous and (albeit apparently successful) self-destructive, and will ultimately render itself extinct. Who cares?

Ulupalakua
July 2006

A LITTLE MORE

I want to share two 'raps' with you that were birthed in 1999 and 2003 respectively, because they're particularly relevant in today's societal climate—so I'm including the preface of the songbook here that you may understand the phenomena:

Revelations of a Sirius Love, and the subsequent collections of Songs, Psalms & Poems presented here, is the result of a boon (Divine Gift) I was offered on the occasion of the re-dedication of my Life and my rebirth as Sahara, in February 1996.

(Thirty years before, at the age of nineteen, I had stepped onto the spiritual path, and after a lifetime dedicated to finding and knowing "God," at the end of 1994 found myself living on the street in Sedona, Arizona. After one-and-a-half years of conditioning, during a personal ceremony conducted by a shaman in a canyon, I rededicated my Life. At the culmination of this life-changing event something extraordinary occurred: I was told that I was being given a *boon*. Feeling that I had already asked for everything I could imagine: a Heart filled with Love, the experience of Oneness, and Service to the Planet; when it was insisted that I request something as a Gift *I heard myself ask for the ability to sing*. Thus was *Sahara* born, and a tap was turned on that is flowing still.

Around the same time, an Indian Master began appearing in my life, intruding himself into my daily experience in a not-at-all subtle way. Having heard of him in the 60's, but having no real understanding of who or what he was, I told him that if I was meant to be with him, he'd have to prove himself to me.

At the end of summer 1998, when I was in an extreme state of desperation, after two full days of screaming at God, asking for direction, the Master called me to India, where he kept me for most of five years—burning in his fire.)

The songs in these volumes were inspired by the amazing Love that started pouring through me, stimulated by my incessant yearning for a merging with my own Self, and at times provoked by various men with whom I had love affairs of diverse natures.

Some express a yearning for romantic love, others a longing for Divine Union. There are those that offer commentary on social consciousness, and others that express the infinite and eternal Love of the Creator, Itself. They all reflect Universal experience and are meant to provoke, inspire, and encourage.

The feeling of a song coming through is a wonderment: exquisite sensations like a current of Love flow through my body, while I am hearing lyric and melody come out of my mouth and watching words appear on a page of my book, written by my hand.

This precious Gift I am sharing here with you.

THE EVOLUTION REVOLUTION/
ONE SOUL, ONE ESSENCE, ONE BEING*

(Rap to a slow groove)

The Evolution Revolution is our only solution
'for we kill ourselves with our insanity
the nuclear madness, environmental sadness
all the actions that deny our Unity—
the Evolution Revolution's what we need

We better recognize the simple truth before we go too far
we better act as if we all, are One—
our possession/obsession has brought us to the brink,
a chain is only strong as—its weakest link,
what makes us think we can progress
as others sink in need,
we are drowning in the quicksand of our greed—
the Evolution Revolution's what we need

We're driving down a lonely road without a spare tire
we're bound by our anger, and by our desire
we've come to a crucial time for the human race:
tinkering with technology can blow us into space
or viruses could kill us all and not leave a trace—
we better face it: we're children with matches,
we are drowning in the quicksand of our greed—
the Evolution Revolution's what we need

Each idea that separates is what we must release
if we want to change our ways and start to live in peace
all worry/pressure/conflict,
comes from 'yours' and 'mine'
Life is a process—it's happening all the time
we *can* do it differently—there *is* a way 'out'
the Evolution Revolution is what it's all about.
who you truly are—who you choose to be
this is the secret that will set us all free—
the Evolution Revolution's what we need

Change yourself and change the world—
the power's in your mind
acknowledgment of Oneness will lead you to find:
everyone is 'you'—just havin' a hard time.
Everyone is 'you'—just wantin' a fair chance,
so wake up! and lighten up! get out of your trance!
you *can* make a difference—we *can* get it right,
we don't have to struggle, we don't have to fight
we are One and there's enough, so let go of your greed—
the Evolution Revolution is what we need

Who you truly are, who you choose to be
is the fuel that drives the engine of change.
if you don't like the way it is, get up off the ground
do the hokey-pokey, and turn yourself around
embody the Consciousness, the sacredness of Life
we don't have to live in fear, or live in stress and strife—
we're *One* Soul, *One* Being, *One* Essence
so open up and step into that Presence
It's the Truth and the Wisdom, of what we're meant to be
give yourself a break, and set your Self free
we are One and there's enough, so let go of your fear
the Evolution Revolution, has started to appear

You are not your body, you are not your mind
you are infinite, eternal—out of space and time
tune into your Consciousness, you will surely see:
pure spirit, the All in All—that is what we be
BE Love, BE Light, BE Kindness
acting like you're not is just blindness
we're *One* Soul, *One* Being, *One* Essence
so open up and step into *your* Presence
It's the Truth and the Wisdom of what we're meant to be
you are **Light**, you are **Love**—set your Self free
we are One and there's enough, so let go of your stuff—
the Evolution Revolution is happenin'—sure enough!!!

*Inspired by the last few chapters of

"Conversations With God" Volume III
By Neale Donald Walsch,
Hampton Roads Publishing, Virginia
Phrases from the book used with permission

Listen here: https://soundcloud.com/siriusgalore

LOVE YOUR NEIGHBOR
(THE POTLATCH SONG)
A Rap

When I'm walkin' in the heat
and a cloud rolls by
I say "thank you"
I say "thank you"

And if I want something to eat
and there's money in my pocket
I say "thank you"
I say "thank you"

This world is like a movie
and we're each assigned a role
sometimes we're Cinderella
sometimes we're Old King Cole

We need to realize
that it's a roll of the dice
sometimes we get Versace
and sometimes we get lice

But what we *do* with what we've got
is what reveals our nature —
are we kind and generous
or nasty and voracious?

To be livin' the good life
is not eating 'til you puke
stop yappin' on that cell phone
can't you see that you've been duped?

The American Dream
has turned into a nightmare—
humanity is in a trance—
it's time to be aware.

When I'm out on the street
and there's someone there who cares
I say "thank you"
I say "thank you"

And when I need a place to sleep
and I have a bed to lie on
I say "thank you"
I say "thank you"

This world is like a movie
and we're each assigned a part
sometimes we get the horse
sometimes we get the cart

We have to understand
that there's something far greater
than crystal chandeliers
and shoes of alligator

What we *do* with what we *have*
will show us who we *are*
will we educate a child
or buy *another* car?

To be livin' the good life
is not eating 'til you puke
Mother Nature's in revolt
and we're being rebuked

The American Dream
has turned into a nightmare
we're like rats—on a treadmill:
moving quickly—going nowhere

We've been brainwashed to believe
too much is not enough
we're consumed by our consumption
we are drowning in our 'stuff'

So open up your eyes, your mind
open up your Heart
let the Love flow to your brother
it's time we made a start

We're the children of One Mother
Love your neighbor as your Self
what we give to each other
is our only true Wealth

Alicante 2003/Agoura 2004
Listen here: https://soundcloud.com/siriusgalore

Source speaks:

Imagine being an ant and encountering an ant the size of a human. Now take that analogy and apply it to humans, but not physically—in terms of Consciousness. The thing that is so amusing about humankind is their arrogance. Their gigantic sense of self. Sure, I gave them dominion over the Earth, but I didn't mean for them to destroy it. I figuratively turned My back for the merest fraction of a second and they had already made a colossal mess of the whole place. Like an untrained puppy, using the living room for a bathroom and tearing things up all over the place, nipping at everybody.

Now I have to restore order in the chaos as gently as possible. It's too lovely a Creation to just throw it in the trash and start again. So I'm moving Higher Consciousness as quickly as possible into the human population so that order may be restored, and My original intention carried out.

Ultimately it will work itself out and Love will triumph—it cannot fail. Of course it might get messy before it's all cleaned up, so don't be too attached to the physical aspect of the character you are playing. My will will be done in the end. My will is prevailing now. Humankind has been designed to express the Love of God.

So it is. And so it shall be.

I have handed out over 5K of these postcards—
this one's for you:

For every time you smile at a 'stranger'—Thank you

For every compliment you give to make someone feel good about themselves—Thank you

For every time you choose the High Road—Thank you

For every act of kindness or service with no need of recognition— Thank you

For every drop of Love you cultivate in your Heart—Thank you

For every ray of Light you send out into the world—Thank you

For every contribution you make for the well-being of All—

Thank you, Thank you, Thank you

S A H A R A
A SERVICE OF SIRIUS-GALORE

Thank you for being
a Contribution
to the

Light

in the world

THE UPLIFT & INSPIRE COLLECTION—SAHARA@SAHARADEVI.COM— INSTAGRAM: SAHARA.SIRIUSGALORE

ABOUT THE AUTHOR

Coming of age in the Sixties, Sahara was fully engaged in the activities of the time, from Anti-war protests to Civil Rights demonstrations; then turned-on, tuned-in, dropped-out and embarked on the Spiritual Path when discovering it was possible to 'know God.' Making this her *raison d'etre*, through the years she has done whatever presented itself to her, experiencing at least three or four different sides of the tracks, from first class to no class.

One of the first group of Yoga Teachers trained by Swami Satchitananda at the IYI in NYC, she served as Mother of the Ashram for five years.

Among other things, she's worked as a Head Start assistant, bank teller, the ubiquitous waitress, freelance photographer and journalist, organic wine salesman, carpenter's assistant and private caterer. She's been a live-in housekeeper for a rock star in Connecticut and a celebrity in Beverly Hills. She's driven a taxi in NYC and a tractor in Israel. In Montana she designed and executed a traffic safety and courtesy campaign, and she sold Japanese yo-yos with her then nine-year-old son on the street in Boulogne, France one Christmas season until they had enough money for dinner each night.

In 1994 she was struck homeless in the same way Ramdass considers he was "stroked"—by an intangible force. One day she was relocating from a northern state to a more desirable clime, a week later she was sleeping in her car, realizing her life would never be the same—embarking on what would become thirteen years of homelessness—first in Sedona and then carried around the world with NVMS, including five unexpected years in India, called telepathically by an Indian Master.

She knows what it is to have to ask for food every time you're hungry, to ask for shelter from the cold at night, and to sleep on a couch in a public library during the day, because you have nowhere else to go. She knows what it is to have a body so weakened by disease that you can barely get up to use the bathroom, have no appetite or even strength to eat, and can only lie in bed, helpless. And she knows what it is to be so broken that if some miracle doesn't save you, you have nothing to live for—the end of the rope.

Sahara has been receiving frequency upgrades of a profound nature over the past few years, including a blast from the Lion's Gate Portal of 8.8.2019, after which she had no need of food for a period of six weeks, living mostly on Light.

Sahara freelanced for the *Good Times* of Sedona; has had a series of articles published in *Yoga Scotland Magazine*; served as Editor of *Spiritual Impressions* magazine in India; and edited the work of Swami Nishchalananda in Wales.

Her previous work: <u>The Evolution Revolution/The First Peaceful Revolution in the World—A Handbook for Personal & Global Transformation</u> (2008) was self-published and sold 500 copies in the USA and the UK. It's currently available as an eBook.

Her book of Songs, Psalms & Poems: <u>The Evolution Revolution: A Journey of Awakening</u> is in the collection at Poets House, NYC.

Of her as yet unpublished autobiography "Awake In The Dream" she says: *Eat, Pray, Love* is to *Awake In The Dream* as *Eloise At The Plaza* is to Homer's *Odyssey*.

She is the creator of The Face of Love™ portrait photography: the face we show to others but never see ourselves, and The Uplift & Inspire Collection—pithy messages in postcard format.

Her life is dedicated to "Transforming the Fabric of Reality for the Well-being of All." She currently resides in Bozeman, Montana.

https://www.saharadevi.com
https://www.facebook.com/sahara.devi
https://www.instagram.com/sahara_sirius.galore
https://www.youtube.com/user/Saharadevi/videos

Promote Unity
Foster Harmony
Love Your Neighbor

THIS IS HOW WE TRANSFORM THE WORLD

SAHARA
A SERVICE OF SIRIUS GALORE

NOW BEGIN...

Made in the USA
Columbia, SC
28 February 2021

33494220R00087